'All the conversations and advi[...]
club toilet, finally in one place'
The *Guardian* Top Ten Comedy Podcasts

'Heart-warmingly honest and beautifully fun,
reading *Keep the Receipts* feels like having
a conversation with a best friend'
Grace Beverley

'There's so much to learn when it comes to being
your own woman and Tolani, Audrey and Milena
aren't afraid to tell you every last detail'
Julie Adenuga

'*Keep the Receipts* is relatable and hilarious.
It gives you the opportunity to see yourself in its pages,
and feel understood on a deeper level'
Ms Banks

'Fiercely funny and unashamedly honest'
Refinery29

'This is the unadulterated "sisterhood" talk that we need'
Stylist

'One of the most carefree, genuine and honest podcasts'
Dazed

'This is a book I would recommend to all women'
The Floor Mag

'A great, easily digestible book packed full of life lessons,
advice and unashamed candidness'
Bad Form

Tolani Shoneye is a podcaster, presenter and writer. She has worked as a beauty and lifestyle writer for various publications and is developing narrative scripted projects for TV. As a host, Tolani has worked with BBC, Netflix and TED. She is a trusted voice that resonates with millennial women, especially Black women.

Audrey Indome is one third of *The Receipts Podcast*. Her passions include discussing social issues, hair, beauty, fashion on a budget and duck jokes! She is a natural conversationalist and aside from the podcast, she has worked as a journalist and radio presenter.

Milena Sanchez is a singer, songwriter and mother. She is best known as the sex positive and big-hearted member of *The Receipts Podcast*. She is passionate and open and is incredibly excited to be making her writing debut alongside Tolani and Audrey.

Keep THE Receipts

TOLANI
SHONEYE

MILENA
SANCHEZ

AUDREY
INDOME

HEADLINE

First published in the UK in 2021 by
HEADLINE PUBLISHING GROUP

First published in paperback in 2022 by
HEADLINE PUBLISHING GROUP

1

Cataloguing in Publication Data is available from the British Library

ISBN 978 1 4722 8258 3

Cover design by Sophie Ellis

Commissioning Editor: Katie Packer
Inside illustrations: Jovilee Burton
Copyeditor: Paula Akpan

Song lyric credit: 'Better Together' by Jack Johnson

Designed and typeset by EM&EN
Printed and bound in Great Britain by Clays Ltd, Elcograf S.p.A.

HEADLINE PUBLISHING GROUP
An Hachette UK Company
Carmelite House
50 Victoria Embankment
London EC4Y 0DZ

www.headline.co.uk
www.hachette.co.uk

Tolly

To all the Black women who have loved me.

Audrey

To my grandmothers, Caroline Chinnery and Teresa Esi Mill.
Caroline lives in Ghana and is one of the kindest and
calmest people you'll ever meet while Teresa gave up her life
in Ghana, as a successful business owner of a shop called
No Regrets, to raise my siblings and me in England.
I would be nothing without them.

Milena

To my beautiful daughter Cataleya Mia,
everything I do is for you. When I was a little girl,
I always wanted to be somebody, and I believed that I was
destined for greatness – I want you to believe that too.
Know that whatever you put your mind to you can achieve,
I wouldn't be the woman I am today without you.
Te amo mi vida x

Contents

Self

Career

Family

Race

Beauty

The Dating Tea

Your Dilemmas Solved

Introduction

It's your girl, Tolly T, Audrey, formally known as Ghana's Finest, and your mamacita, Milena Sanchez – AAAOOOWWWWW and welcome to our book. We can't believe that's a thing we are actually saying, or writing even! A book written by us and about us – what a long way we have come from starting a podcast as strangers to now having written a book together.

This book is not intended to be a self-help book. Think of it more as an episode of *Your Receipts*; you know the episodes where we help you out with your dilemmas, predicaments and situationships? But this time, the dilemmas are our own, the predicaments involve our pain and the situationships (unfortunately) are from our pasts. This book is filled with our highlights and lowlights – we write about our relationships, our families, our lives, and often, those weird thoughts that float about in our heads too. We don't claim to have worked everything out, but we have learned a lot from our experiences, and we hope you get something out of them too. The 'three women, real talk, no filter' is not just a jazzy slogan for the cover; it can also be read as a warning. These pages are filled with our truths and we do not take responsibility for any feelings hurt or egos bruised.

If you have never heard of the podcast and are just here because the cover caught your attention and the thought of three women talking candidly excites you then welcome, you're in for a great ride. Imagine you've just met us in the girls' toilets; we're those friends you make in five minutes over a cocktail or eight. You're lucky, once you've gobbled up the book, you have tonnes of episodes to fill the void it leaves. And if you've been with us from the very beginning and have been religiously tuning in every week, thank you. You are truly the best and we hope this book allows you to know us deeper.

The three of us met in 2016 after Tolly put out a call on Twitter that read: 'I have a podcast name, now I just need the girls.' The podcast name *Cocktails and Cock Tails* quickly left the scene, but the girls stayed. To say we anticipated any success would be a lie – we just wanted to have a chat, to form a space where we could provide a little social commentary and a lot of straight talking.

Cocktails and Cock Tails was among a long list of names that just didn't work out, *Can't Deal* was in the running and so was *Pre-Drinks*, all pretty awful podcast names if we're being honest. But *The Receipts Podcast* stuck. The name was inspired by a Whitney Houston interview with Diane Sawyer, RIP to a true legend (Whitney that is,

Diane Sawyer is still alive). After Diane asked Whitney about her alleged drug abuse, Whitney replied, 'Where are the receipts, show me the receipts. Where is the evidence that I'm doing this?' And we thought, well, we're giving our evidence, we're giving our side of the story on the podcast and we're platforming all of your receipts too, so we agreed on the name *The Receipts Podcast*.

This book, *Keep the Receipts*, is honest, it's brave and it's unfiltered. We hope our podcast listeners read the chapters in our individual voices and that it gives you a better idea of who we are, what we think and feel and what we have learned so far in this mad life. The chapters are based on topics that we hold dearly, topics that shaped us. So, whoever you are, we hope that this book makes you laugh, allows you to feel seen and above all, we hope it keeps you company.

Tolly

I am a rookie on love. Everything I know about it is from what I have seen in movies, what I have heard in love songs and what I imagine it to be. I am a rookie on love because I am afraid of it; I'm afraid of its force, and I am afraid of my thirst for it. The love of my imagination feels good – it's safe, it keeps my secrets, it soothes me, it makes life easier and it makes life beautiful. It feels like a Sunday morning. A Sunday morning that was crafted just for me. One where I have woken up to the smell of yam and egg stew, a smell that ignites the same feeling in me that you might get from the sweet scent of cinnamon rolls or homemade bread. I thought I should add that comparison in case you have not lived life to the fullest and are yet to experience Sundays with yam and egg stew.

On this dreamy Sunday morning, I have woken up at my own leisure, thanked God for another day and, on the other side of the bed, I can make out the impression left by his body, the slight indentations that mark that spot as his. The weather is perfect. We eat breakfast, made by him, and then we head to church. Praise and worship goes off without a bad note and the sermon is both touching and motivating. We head to brunch, and, of course, stop by the flower shop before going home. Just when we get home it starts to rain and we giggle as we run into the house for shelter. I change into my pyjamas and him into his grey tracksuit and vest. We spend the rest of the day cuddling. Naturally, Mariah Carey's 'Always Be My Baby' provides the soundtrack. This is the love of my imagination, and this love feels like home.

But the love of my past has been very different to this. The love I have experienced has quite frankly been an emotional, financial and physical journey through hell, very far removed from my imagined Sunday morning. It was a love I knew I was better than and, deep down under the layers of self-hate, I knew that I deserved more than that version of love. You see, for me, love and everything that comes with it exists in two worlds: one that is healthy and the other that is unhealthy. And, to add to the complexities of love, I don't know if these two are mutually exclusive.

Unhealthy love for me has no rationale. It leads with possession. It has this tendency to make excessive and unrealistic demands. It's this idea that your lover needs to be your everything. This love is often hidden under the disguise of passion. This was the notion of love that I had. My first love came hand in hand with intensity, ownership and volatility. I gave it my all, believing that that was what you did when you were in love, but I never felt loved back. I kept showing more love in the hope that it would be reciprocated. I longed for the day when my love would be appreciated, where it would be seen as something that was valuable, something that needed to be nurtured.

I assumed love meant that you stayed through it all, even when 'it all' was disrespect, betrayal and hurt. I assumed that true love neglected the self and put the other person first. I got caught up in what that love felt like when it first started and not what it evolved into. What it evolved into wasn't healthy – I loved too hard. I know, I, too, rolled my eyes after writing those words. People often describe loving too hard as some sort of adorable personality trait of the sensitive ones of the world, the ones with huge hearts. Those of us that claim to love too hard are caring, we put our partners first, we take pride in the way we love, and we are most satisfied when we are pouring our love out to other people, regardless of whether they give it back to us. But this means we are often not fed. We give our love to people who are undeserving. Everything about my first love was unhealthy, and it was a love that ended in heartbreak.

Those who have been heartbroken know I am not exaggerating when I say it feels like you're dying. It's a feeling that you think you'll never get over. Nothing feels comforting and all the coping mechanisms you've heard about don't work. No amount of going out and wearing less makes it better, it hurts. During my heartbreak, I felt waves of pain, anger and withdrawal. I knew that the relationship needed to end, yet I had this desire to get another hit. I wanted to make it work; I wanted to see my ex and talk to him. This was someone I had been with for ten years and the end of our relationship meant that he was no longer alive in my life; I had to grieve this loss.

I have never known how to block or suppress my feelings, so I felt every part of this pain, with my heart shattered. Getting over this was not easy. Trying to put yourself back together after being broken is so hard. I don't think there's a step-by-step guide to getting over heartbreak, regardless of all the articles that claim to know the answer and yes, I googled it. Through teary eyes, I typed into that Google search bar 'how to get over a break-up'. No result that came up stopped the pain. What worked was time, until one day I just wasn't sad any more.

I learned a lot from this love. It was in its ending that I learned that I needed to love myself. Throughout that relationship I wasn't kind to myself. Everyone shouts about self-love as if it's a thing that just happens or a skill everyone is meant to have, but no one tells you how hard it is and how it takes a conscious effort. Loving yourself has to be purposeful and it's something you have to keep working on – it's consistent. Being able to unapologetically love myself doesn't mean that I have no insecurities or that I am happy with all of me all of the time, it just means that I love myself despite the bits I don't like. Self-love makes me more capable of having healthy romantic relationships. I feel whole, which means I don't crave external validation. I love myself enough to know I am deserving of a great love, just like my perfect Sunday morning.

My heartbreak also taught me how to deal with rejection because to be dumped is to be rejected; you are no longer wanted. Rejection was not new to me at this point but it still hurt so much. The first boy I ever fancied rejected me. I had never pined for someone as deeply as I pined for Callum in primary school. Everything about him was perfect to me. Although he wore the same white polo, grey trousers and red jumper stamped with the same William Ford Primary School logo as everyone else, I was sure he wore his differently – he made it look better. I had spent so much time looking at him that I could have told you the number of freckles he had on his face, it was around thirty-two if I remember correctly. I wanted to be the kind of girl that he would like but, for Callum, blonde girls who could get their hair up without the help of a wide-tooth comb were his type. So, no matter how much I wanted it, Callum was not going to fancy me back.

Every time I got rejected, I blamed it on all the things I lacked. With Callum, I thought that maybe if I was prettier he would like me back. With this ex, I considered how he may have wanted to stay in the relationship if I loved him better and that maybe, just maybe, if I was a little less me, he would have chosen to stay. But this focus on what I lacked meant I never really saw what I had. I had to see myself through my eyes and not through the lens of those who had rejected me. I couldn't convince them to see my worth, but I sure as hell needed to convince myself of it. I started appreciating what I had and started to love the components that make me, me. I centred my focus on me and I promised myself that I wasn't going to allow my bad experiences to taint love. Love meant too much to me to allow anyone outside of me to ruin it.

I love 'love' so much that I have the word tattooed on my body. Everything about me is centred around love. Love for me is the closest thing we have to magic because the odds of finding the truest version of it are against us. The world is filled with billions of people who are raised differently and who see the world differently, so to find someone who you love, to love them how they want to be loved and for that same person to love you the way you long to be loved is truly magical. I cannot make sense of love because it feels much bigger than me and, for someone who loves love so much, I feel very let down by it. I have never known a love that feels exclusive to me, the love that comes from an intimate relationship. I don't know what it feels like to be someone's one and only. I have never felt a love that soothes my fear of loneliness or that comes with safety. I have experienced rich and fulfilling love that lives outside of romantic relationships, but this doesn't quieten my desire for eros love. I desire closeness and intimacy. I don't want to live a life where I am OK to miss out on this. I can't afford to give up on this idea of love because I don't know what life looks like if I am denied this experience and I don't want to know.

> Love for me is the closest thing we have to magic because the odds of finding the truest version of it are against us.

My longing for romantic love is often seen as a weakness and a need for co-dependency. It is met with 'you need to love yourself.' But this is not about my lack of self-love. I love me and I know my value now but from when I was young, I had dreams of meeting the love of my life and living our version of happily ever after. I don't believe that we are meant to be alone, and I refuse to shame myself or allow others to shame me for this very human want; to be loved. The connection that comes with romantic love is of great importance to me because it's a safe space where you can share your joy and sadness. It's having your own personal person. Regardless of how unkind love has been to me, I can't numb myself to it. My need for love overrides my fear of pain. I cherish this part of me and I see it as one of my best bits.

I love love stories. I get enveloped in people's tales about their greatest love. I watch movies about it and I read books about it. But my favourite story of them all is my own; this story is about the greatest love I have felt for someone. Now, this is not a love of my imagination, it's a love that is real and one that I feel deeply. Everything about this love feels like Brandy's 'Almost Doesn't Count', or more accurately Tamia's 'Almost'. It's not a crush, I am familiar with them, I have had plenty of them, this is love. I have written many love stories about him; it is his image I imagine when I listen to love songs. My love for him doesn't overwhelm me, it calms me. It's the safety of being wrapped up in a blanket but also the freedom of rolling a car window down, sticking my head out of it and letting the breeze hit me. It's the closest thing I have felt to healthy love. I am truthful and candid with him without fear of judgement, I willingly give up my ugly truths. It gives me all the things I ask for from love.

I am sure like me, you have been told to write a list, a list of all the things you want or are looking for from love. I have written and rewritten a list often and this is the most recent version. At my very core, these are the things I expect from my version of healthy love:

* A love that gives me the freedom to be me, where I can exist as the whole version of me. I need my life to be centred around me, and this love needs to live alongside that. I like support and encouragement but I don't need a partner to be involved in every part of my life. This is the same freedom I hope to give my partner.

* A love that is built on trust. I don't want to question where I fit into this person's life. Nor do I want to question the person's intentions, we are a team, and we move like one. My love is my G, and having a G comes with the confidence of someone always having your back.

* I crave a love that's balanced. One where everyone is playing their role and both our needs are met. I understand the need for compromise, and I know there may be times when more is expected from one person, but I never want the burden to feel too much to carry for either of us.

Tolly

*   I want a kind love, a kindness that is given and returned. One that shows compassion, one that is generous and considerate.

*   I demand respect from a relationship because healthy love for me has boundaries, boundaries that are respected and regarded. I am not of the belief that this love is conflict-free. I know conflict is inevitable when two people who have lived very different lives come together. And I don't think it's always a bad thing. Yes, it comes with anger and discomfort, but it encourages honest conversations. I know I am not above the classic 'fuck you' and 'I hate you' but I want to aim for healthy conflict. One that recognises the problems at their roots, and, of course, the romantic part of me would like the conflict to end in make-up sex.

*   I need this love to be fun and fun should be injected into our daily routines. I want to laugh often, have private jokes and find pleasure in spending time together. I want a love that curates a friendship beyond the romantic and sexual connection.

*   I want a love that is romantic, a romance according to us.

That's not too much to ask for, right?

Audrey

Someone once asked me what I think love means and I had no clue how to respond. I guess I never really thought about how to quantify or verbalise it, I just knew it as an unexplainable feeling that could bring out the best and worst in you. People say that, for women, the first man we fall in love with is our father. I often think about how my relationship with my dad has shaped who I am today and how my love for him has impacted my view on love overall. I've always had a great relationship with my dad and we're very similar in many ways.

My mum moved to England by herself as a young nineteen year old ready to train as a nurse. She left my dad behind in Ghana to pursue this dream of hers but when she discovered she was pregnant with me, my dad dropped everything and moved to London to be there for his family. They both did menial jobs to make ends meet and eventually got married when I was five. When I think about the sacrifices my parents made, it can be overwhelming. I often think about how hard they worked just so that I could have a completely different experience to them – where I could be a nineteen year old whose only concerns would be university, friends and my social life. This is the type of love I hope I can pass on to my future children one day. I saw a version of love in my parents' marriage which was always filled with fun and enjoyment. I remember, after being sent to bed as a kid, not being able to fall asleep because of the sounds of my mum and dad's roaring laughter in the front room of our flat. In my young mind, I realised that a couple who laughed together would stay together.

> I saw a version of love in my parents' marriage which was always filled with fun and enjoyment.

However, I was also conflicted when I thought about love because the love I'd see on TV was a different version to what my parents had. On TV, it looked like big displays of affection, kissing each other goodbye at the door before work and hearing 'I love you' constantly. I felt love all around me, but it wasn't like this. Love was there in the Ghanaian music played in our flat on the weekends while my parents reminisced about their childhoods and what each song meant to them. Love was there when my younger sister and I would climb into my mum and dad's bed every Saturday morning and pester them about what we were doing that day. I rarely heard the words 'I love you' exchanged between my mum and dad but I just knew it was there, I felt it.

This helped me learn quite early on the difference between what was real and what wasn't, and I decided that what

I saw on TV wasn't. How could it be? The real-life examples I had in front me made the TV examples seem like make-believe. This has had a huge impact on how I see love now, especially as I'm quite logical and practical and believe the strength of the partnership is more important than affection. This disconnect between love at home and the styles of love seen in the media is a common experience growing up in African homes. I believe it stems from the idea of marriage being a partnership and something you do to build a legacy, rather than doing it for love – something that seems to be changing with Millennials and Gen Z.

A therapist once said to me that we learn patterns of how to love through what we saw with our parents growing up, the same way they learned through their parents and so on. When I think specifically about how my dad loved us, I realise it was a choice. My grandfather, rest his soul, was a complicated but wonderful man and I assume he did his best for my dad and his siblings. From whispers, I knew that he was an excellent provider, he kept his home immaculate, he made sure school fees were always paid and he put clothes on everyone's back. However, unfortunately, he lacked the ability to be emotional and could be quite cold and disconnected. My dad learned from this experience and decided to go in the opposite direction with his family, showering my siblings and me in love and affirmations. My dad has been a direct bridge to who I've chosen to be with because I saw so many qualities in him that set an example of what I'd want in a man. The most important of these is being a kind person and owning it. My dad showed me that being masculine doesn't mean being angry or assertive but, instead, demonstrated that you could be warm, kind and approachable, still lead a household and obtain the utmost respect.

✧

I've spoken about my eternal crush a million times on the podcast, and they shall remain unnamed in print, but honestly my love – or obsession – began at the age of four in reception. Yes really, that young. Puppy love and early childhood crushes are often undermined but I think it's high time we start putting some respect on their name because that shit is as real as married love at thirty-four . . . OK, I'm exaggerating but I definitely believe there's something in it. Most importantly, I think your character is shaped by whether that love is reciprocated or not, and it influences how you go on to love in the future.

My love was, in fact, not reciprocated (not that I ever told him). I spent a lot of time observing who he was attracted to, i.e. who he 'went out with' and who he ran after during kiss chase. I realised quickly that none of those girls looked like me and so I knew straight away I didn't stand a chance. I was one of the only Black girls in my class and, inevitably, I stood out from the rest: my hair was different, my skin was different and, even that young, I could see what perceived beauty looked like simply based on who all the boys fancied. As a Black girl in a predominantly white school, you don't know you're different until someone tells you, and although I don't remember many obvious incidents where my difference was pointed out, I do remember feeling invisible when it came to attraction and the boys I fancied. I recall specifically telling myself out loud to put boys on the back burner because no one was going to fancy me. I was ten.

Once I'd decided love wasn't going to be my bag, I focused my energy on school and being a high achiever. I wasn't naturally intelligent, but I was a hard worker. I consider myself lucky to have taken on this mindset so young because I've heard so many stories of young girls going in the opposite direction and doing anything to feel love from the opposite sex. I think, subconsciously, I had decided to focus on my personality. I wasn't aware at the time that this was what I was doing but I was friend-zoned so much, it taught me how to build relationships with men that weren't romantic. It allowed me the opportunity to observe people at a young age, so I was able to determine what I did and didn't want in a relationship. I didn't know this would help me in the future.

Now that I've told you about my first love, it's only right I tell you about my first heartbreak; unfortunately, the two often come together. My first heartbreak was tragic and dramatic, and though it was someone who I wasn't even interested in at first, boy did I grow to love this guy. He'd just moved to the UK from Jamaica and had an amazing thick accent. Every day I'd walk home from school and, without fail, he'd shout, 'Audrey, when you gonna be my girl?' Because I was quite insecure at the time and had become so accustomed to not being found attractive, I thought it was just banter. However he was persistent and eventually I gave in to him. We were boyfriend and girlfriend for all of two months.

The first time I felt actual pain because of love was when I found out he slept with a friend of mine. I cried so hard, I literally couldn't breathe. I don't know what upset me more: the fact it was a friend or the fact he cheated. All I know is that I felt so depressed and miserable that I sat at the top the stairs and sobbed so hard, my mum heard. I grew up in a pretty strict African household where boys were pretty much forbidden so when I heard my mum coming, I wiped away my tears and tried to get myself together, but it was too late. My mum asked me what was wrong and I lied, but a mother always knows. She asked me again and, after I told her what had happened, she held my chin and said 'Audrey, darling, this will be the first of many tears you will cry over a man, wipe the tears away, you'll be fine.' I was pleasantly surprised – I'd never imagined confiding in my mum about man problems but, in that moment, I think she was the only person who could comfort me.

Heartbreak, and how to get over it, is a question we get asked all the time on the podcast and I really wish there was a magic pill or remedy that could make it go away. I remember watching an episode of *Insecure* and Issa Rae said, 'Men don't heal, they hoe' and honestly, I couldn't agree more. I believe men and women handle break-ups and heartbreaks very differently. When a relationship ends, women tend to go through 'the process'; we cry all the tears until we have nothing left, we feel all our feelings until we're numb and then one day we wake up and realise we have to move on and accept it's over. Men, on the other hand, deal with heartbreak by boning everything in sight, hoping to forget the pain. They go out with their boys and try and enjoy themselves but then reality hits them. That's when you get the 'hey stranger' text.

I know that for me, the concept of getting under someone new to get over someone old has never worked; I've tried and it failed miserably. What I've learned through experience is that you *will* get over it, even though it feels like the end of the world. In the moment, it's like you can't function, can't concentrate at work (I've called in sick so many times due to heartbreak) and all you want to do is wallow in self-pity and cry all day long. I promise you, it's all normal and it will pass. During some of my worst heartbreaks, I remember trying to keep myself busy by taking on new hobbies, but I quickly learned that you're simply putting a plaster on an open wound. Allow yourself a couple of days to feel sorry for yourself. Take a personal day from work and just feel – you'll soon find you have no more tears left to cry. Going through the process and not forcing myself, or pretending, to be OK helped me massively and it is one of the best practical tips I can give on how to deal with love lost.

Even if you're the person doing the dumping, you're still bound to feel pain. A break-up lowkey feels like a death and, on some level, you're mourning the loss of that relationship and that person. Guilt is something that can eat you up when you're the dumper. As women, the pressure to settle down and find the one is so intense that God forbid you decide you don't want to be in something any more, especially when you're in your thirties. However, if you're strong in your conviction and what you want the trajectory of your life to look like, you have to block out all the background noise and do what's right for you. I'm glad the definition of what it means to be selfish seems to be shifting and it's no longer seen as just a negative thing. Selfishness can be vital to self-development and there will be times in your life – not just when it comes to love but other parts too – that you'll have to put yourself first.

> Selfishness can be vital to self-development and there will be times in your life – not just when it comes to love but other parts too – that you'll have to put yourself first.

Love has been one hell of a rollercoaster for me. I've always wondered whether you can choose love or not. Sometimes I think that how love works out for you is down to how you manifest it but other times, I think it is a ball of uncontrollable feelings that makes you feel super high at best and insanely low at worst. I still don't have the answer and I don't know if I ever will. The first time I knew I felt real love was with my university boyfriend, who I was on and off with for five years, and I learned so much from that situation. It's what I would describe as my first grown-up relationship because I was able to see him freely without the eyes of my mum and dad in my business. Living on campus afforded me freedom that I would've never had still living at home. This was the first time I was in love and I knew it wasn't puppy love or a crush because, for one, it was reciprocated – well, sometimes – and secondly, it felt serious. This was the first time I said 'I love you' and the story makes me cringe because he didn't say it back . . . awks! It was also the first time that I was having regular sex. One of the biggest things I learned from that relationship was that you can be on two totally different pages with someone you're with. As troubled as our relationship was, at the tender age of twenty-two, I was convinced I was going to marry this guy. I thought I had it all figured out. Sometimes you forget that there's so much more life to live. One thing I always say to young women in their early twenties is to focus on yourself. Live your best life; travel and enjoy yourself because it goes by so fast. As hard as it is to go against the grain, especially if you've had marriage drummed into your head from a young age as many West African girls do, I promise you there's plenty of time to settle down – enjoy the now.

When I met Nick, I'd recently become single again after yet another failed talking stage. I wasn't in the best of places because I was traumatised from my last relationship. I had made a vow to stay single and focus on my career, which was dwindling because I had spent too much energy chasing men all over town. I was mean and cold, the total opposite of who I am, but previous experiences had hardened me. I don't know how but Nick saw through that façade and stuck around until I defrosted. He said 'I knew that's not who you were.' Nick's patience was such a learning curve for me and it was the first relationship I had been in where I felt relaxed. He consistently showed he was different; he put me first always and, because of this, I let my guard down. Fast-forward ten years, we got engaged, moved in together and planned two huge weddings in the space of two years.

I always get asked for marriage advice or to speak on being married as the only one in the podcast who is and I often say 'I don't have the answers because I haven't been doing this long enough to advise anyone yet.' As much as I enjoy being married and it is a huge part of who I am, I've tried to distance myself from making it my whole 'brand'. I think it's important to decide if you want to be a married woman or a woman who's married – that's if you choose to get married at all. As a woman it's so easy for your identity to get wrapped up in who you're partnered with, and although I was proud and happy to be married, I didn't want it to be all that I was. I wanted to be an individual who contributes to a partnership. I don't know if this is the correct mentality to have in a marriage and this might be part of the reason why we separated in 2020. I often get asked what it was about Nick that made me decide to say yes. There are a million things I could list but the key ones are his emotional intelligence, empathy and ability to express himself and communicate. Having lost his mother at the age of ten and his father suddenly at twenty-five, which I was by his side for, I think it made Nick view life differently and grow up a lot faster than his age mates – something that was also evident in our relationship. I could speak all day on our relationship but often, I have to reign myself in and remember it's not just my story to be told.

When it comes to love, all in all, I'd say it's been good to me and I feel privileged to have experienced the good, the bad and the ugly that comes with it. However, I think love and relationships don't always go hand in hand. Love is risk, love is uncertainty and love feels mind-blowing, whereas relationships are work – they are hard and testing. So how do you combine all these elements that are so juxtaposed? It's a challenge for sure.

From my father's love, to my first crush in primary school, to my first heartbreak, to my first real love and right through to my husband, there is one thing that remains true: you learn something new from each love you experience. Self-refection in love is important so that you can learn from your mistakes. Self-love is also important because it's impossible to love someone without also loving yourself. Boundaries are also key; identifying how you want to be loved so you can recognise if someone isn't giving you what you need. I've seen far too many women sacrifice their wants and desires for people who are not willing to do the same – it's OK to leave a relationship that isn't serving you. Romantic love doesn't have to be unconditional. I think this is a myth that is sold to women to keep us in our place and strip us of agency over ourselves. Love should be what feels right for you as an individual, based on your own personal wants and needs, and once that special someone can meet you somewhere in the middle, I promise you, you'll be just fine.

✧

Milena

I have always loved love. I'm that girl who stupidly gives guys 'one more chance' (times that by a hundred) because there is always a chance they could change, right? *Wrong*. Still, it has never stopped me from moving on to the next one, as Jay-Z would say. The thing is I'm someone who wears my heart on my sleeve and, although sometimes I wish I could shove it in a cage, lock it away and throw the key out, I've learned a hell of a lot about love. Plus, it has given me some crazy shit to talk about.

See, the problem I have is that the moment I meet somebody, I let my imagination run away with my heart. I could honestly fall in love with someone who innocently opened a door for me. As you can imagine, this habit of mine is a shortcut to hurt and disappointment when things do not go as planned – something that happens a lot more than I'd like to admit. Over time, this constant feeling of being let down in love left me feeling drained. I started wondering if my perception of love was realistic and if it was ever worth having such high expectations of people. I now realise that it's not always going to be fireworks and butterflies and that is OK, but I still wish I knew people's intentions from the get-go to stop me getting too far ahead of myself. I mean, if I had it my way it would just be simple – I don't think I want too much! When I think of my future, I see myself married to the love of my life in our beautiful home that we've worked hard to get, we're financially stable and have beautiful kids. But every time I think I've found 'the one' that fits

> The problem I have is that the moment I meet somebody, I let my imagination run away with my heart.

perfectly into this image I have of my future, something always seems to go wrong and I'm left back at square one. My soulmate's probably lying next to his girlfriend as we speak but anyways.

Like with all stories, it's best to start at the beginning, and for me that means my first childhood love. Oh how I miss those Trocadero nights, park strolls and racing to the house phone every time it rang to make sure I got to it before my mum, just in case it was him. It was all so innocent. This was the first time I experienced the romance I had grown up watching on TV. It was a time when I realised that I loved the small shit that had sentimental value and that, maybe, just maybe, the complete fairy-tale of a man that I had seen in all the novelas wasn't so unobtainable after all. In my head (key word being 'my'), we had been together for a couple of years and when I walked into my quinceañera (a celebration of a girl's fifteenth birthday in

Latin America) with him holding my hand, I felt like it was my wedding day. I was the happiest girl in the world. That was until I found out that he was also drawing sweet Winnie the Pooh illustrations for another girl.

To say 'I was devastated' would be an understatement. I remember that dramatic break-up like it was yesterday: the crying to LeAnn Rimes' 'How Do I Live' and even more sobbing my heart out while going through the drawer of all of the cute things he had given me. It was the first time I had experienced heartbreak and feeling like another girl was better than me, like I wasn't enough. Sadly, that feeling was consistent throughout most of my relationships. Over time, I realised that this came from my childhood, rather than this relationship – but we'll get to that later.

After my childhood love came my first proper love. I can still vividly remember the first time I came across Kyle: the man I spent almost nine years with, the man that ended up being my best friend, and the man who became the father to my child. It was 31 October and I was at my aunty's Halloween party. I was upstairs on the computer talking to my friends on Facebook because, having just turned seventeen, I thought I was too cool to hang with the kids at the party and too young to be with the adults. I was scrolling through his friend's page who I met through college when I came across a picture of him. I just knew I had to have him; I loved his smile, his hair, his eyes and I was elated that he was tagged. I added him, he accepted, and we started talking straight away. From a young age, I'd always felt confident enough to approach men as I've never wanted to let a potential opportunity of being in love slide. Yes, rejection has been hard at times but, for me, it's always about throwing myself in at the deep end and taking that chance even if it doesn't amount to anything. I didn't mind loving and losing.

Things escalated pretty quick with Kyle and by the second week of dating, I asked him to be my boyfriend, which he reluctantly agreed to. We spent most days together and he became my all – to the point where it was an unhealthy kind of obsession. I didn't want to go out or spend a night away from him and I'd feel deeply offended if he wanted his space – it triggered the four-year-old me who knew how it felt to be left and abandoned. We ended up taking a break for a month just so we could regain our independence outside of the relationship and I honestly thought I was going to die, *no joke*. I wasn't eating or sleeping, and everything reminded me of him, but as the weeks went on, it got easier. It was the best thing we could have done because, from there, we ended up balancing everything around us pretty well.

When we first got together, I had brushed off a few things that I knew I wasn't OK with because I didn't want to lose him. For example, I had to pretend that I was OK with minimal affection when, really, I wanted to be embraced and feel loved. The small things soon built up to be a huge weight on our relationship and I learned the hard way that communication is key – you should never have to fear pointing out issues in your relationship. There were many times where it all got too much and I can still remember my heart hurting from the ache caused by crying. In my mind, there was no way I was going to be without this man. I loved him to death and though some days I wanted to kill him (joking . . .), I could never ever picture my life without him. Hindsight is a beautiful thing and now looking back, I realise I was a lost seventeen year old, desperately craving the stable male figure that had been absent when I was growing up. Kyle gave me that consistency, love, friendship and security which meant that if I felt like he was going to leave, it was the end of the world to me.

We had been together for seven years when I fell pregnant and there was no question of whether or not we wanted to keep the baby – in fact three years prior to getting pregnant we watched a film called *Colombiana,* and after hearing the name for the first time we decided we wanted to call our future daughter Cataleya and I spoke her into existence. Pregnancy was tough for the both of us emotionally, but physically I was feeling most of the effects as I was growing his whole big-headed child inside of me along with all the hormones hitting me hard. The one event that really rocked our world and our pregnancy experience, and made us brush our relationship issues under the carpet, was when Kyle's younger brother Tyrell was involved in a life-changing car accident. It was a matter of life or death and nothing else mattered but him. I was five months pregnant at the time and we had to wait in the ICU for information. Tyrell had been airlifted to St Mary's Hospital in Paddington, so we knew this wasn't a small accident. I will never forget the cries that came from the room that the doctor had taken Tyrell's parents and Kyle into, they will probably follow me forever.

The doctor told us his injuries meant that he would not survive as he had suffered serious trauma to the brain. I didn't know how to be there for Kyle in this time, but I tried. I had to bury my feelings and just make sure he was OK. The following forty-eight hours were critical, there was a chance they could operate and save him but they didn't know what kind of quality of life he would have. However, because he had two beautiful daughters the family felt they had to try and save him, even if the chances of him surviving were slim. Having my baby in me and feeling her flutter around comforted me but I couldn't help but feel bad for the amount of emotions and anxiety running through my body that could be impacting her.

After Tyrell's operation, we had to take each day as it came which was soul destroying because we all feared the unknown. The family spent every day by Tyrell's side all the way up until I gave birth. Thankfully, Tyrell survived, however we neglected everything around the pregnancy as his life was the focus – this wasn't your fault Tyrell if you're reading, it's just life and we love you! I can't lie though, I was at my loneliest back then which wasn't how I'd imagined my first pregnancy to be and, for many years after, I was full of resentment. From the moment I found out I was pregnant to actually giving birth, we brushed so many difficulties under the rug that once we settled down a bit, it all exploded.

I couldn't believe it: I had given who I thought was the love of my life the biggest gift a woman and God could give and still I felt like I wasn't worthy. I'll admit that we both made mistakes. I know whole-heartedly if we could go back, there would be a lot that we'd change but that means nothing now. We really tried making things work for Cataleya but we both knew we'd work better as friends. It was so strange as there wasn't ever a final conversation, we were on and off for a couple of years until we just knew it wasn't going anywhere. We were scared because we were all we knew but we also didn't want it getting toxic in the end. It wasn't ideal as I felt like I had failed my daughter but, in reality, I hadn't at all. He's the best dad in the world, and I'm glad my child hasn't had to grow up in the tense and damaging environment of our relationship had it continued, just because we wanted her to have both parents under one roof.

Despite being a wreck every time I watched Cataleya and her dad together (on some level, I was jealous), it makes me feel so content to know that she is able to experience something I never had. What I had learned from this almost decade-long relationship was that I shouldn't measure my value by men's opinions of me – if you live by a man's compliments, you'll die by his criticism. I'll never in my life love a man that way again. It was that stupid love; that I-would-do-anything-to-keep-you kind of love; that

I-will-compromise-whatever-it-is-just-to-make-sure-you-are-happy kind of love and, you know what? I'm not on it. I now know (as cliché as it may sound) that you need to love yourself first before getting into any relationship. I don't believe for a second this man didn't love me, I know he did and does, but the way we communicated our love wasn't how either one of us wanted to receive it. Love languages are real and if someone is not willing to learn your love then it's not worth it.

I knew I had to keep in mind all of the lessons I had learned in my past relationship for my next relationship and, a few years later, I found the next lucky guy (after momentarily dating fuckboys, being a little side ting for a bit by accident, and entertaining guys I just wasn't fully into). It was the first time I had ever called another man my boyfriend since the age of seventeen and that was a scary thought. There were new challenges that came with loving someone new, like trying to blend a family. It was definitely a challenge and I really tried my best to do what was right for Cataleya. He didn't meet her until we had been together way over a year and I made sure he met her dad prior to that. I tried to make everybody feel as comfortable as possible before taking such a huge step and, most importantly, I wanted to make sure my daughter came before anything else. I was sceptical and afraid of the time they spent together as I still wasn't sure if this was 'it' though I wanted it to be so badly. He met so many needs that other guys never did so I tried to make it work with everything in me, without his knowledge. The sad thing is my 'needs' were the bare minimum; being shown off, simply feeling wanted and loved, all originating, yet again, from the psychological effects of an absent male figure.

He was great – with me, with Cataleya, and with my family. I had never had a man show me love like that and yet, there was still something missing and I couldn't put my finger on it. All the women around me loved how attentive and thoughtful he was and never failed to remind me how lucky and blessed I was. The thing is, this sent my anxiety through the roof because I kept thinking there was something wrong with me. How could I not be head over heels with somebody as loving and caring as him? I finally had a man who was ready to make me his wife and now I was running away? How was that even possible? From the outside looking in, everybody thought we were perfect and loved us together, but my closest around me would always say 'Milena, you can't just stay because he's a nice person.' The truth was I had been hurt so much in the past that I thought if I left him, I'd never come across a man willing to love me again. I was, once again, letting my fears get the better of me.

I began going to therapy as I needed some guidance – I was ready to face the demons I kept locked away from my past. Ten weeks in and it was like I had a self-discovery that made me really come to terms with everything. It changed my life for the better and I was forced to acknowledge everything I tried to suppress. I realised I had to end that relationship. Though I knew breaking up was the right thing, guilt and fear kept me there longer because I didn't want to hurt somebody so sweet. But the truth is, I wasn't 100% happy and I had to be true to myself and to him. Finally, I could differentiate between self-sabotaging and something just not being for me. Still, it was fucking hard ending things. Regardless, I went through this break-up feeling like I knew myself and what I actually wanted. It was the first break-up that I was able to accept, not because I didn't have love for him, but because I knew morally it the best for the both of us if I was just open and honest. I had gone down the road of trying to brush things off in the past and I knew I couldn't put myself through that again. I don't regret the relationship or see it as a waste of two years, I just finally came into myself and, for once, I had clarity.

Despite all this, I still love love. The most important love that I have discovered that isn't going anywhere is my love for Hazel Milena Sanchez. I've learnt that I can never leave me and so I better make it a happy relationship. I've also learnt that love is both painful and beautiful. One minute you could feel like your whole world is crashing down and then the next, you feel like you're the happiest person in the world. However, one thing is for sure in all of this – there is always new dick right around the corner.

✧

TOLLY'S LIFE IN A ROMCOM

AT THE PREMIERE SCREENING OF TOLLY'S FIRST TV SHOW SHE'S SCREEN-WRITTEN, TOLLY'S MAN IS IN THE AUDIENCE. HE RAISES HIS HAND TO ASK A QUESTION, AND STANDS UP IN THE CROWD:

I DON'T HAVE A QUESTION. I JUST WANT TO SAY, I'M YOUR BIGGEST FAN.

DURING A DATE IN THE PARK, TOLANI DECIDES SHE WANTS TO LEARN TO RIDE A BIKE. HER MAN GETS HER THE BIKE AND BEGINS TO TEACH HER, BUT JUST WHEN SHE IS GETTING THE HANG OF IT, SHE FALLS TO THE GROUND. HE RUNS TO HER RESCUE AND SHE PULLS HIM DOWN ONTO THE GRASS AS THEY GIGGLE AND KISS.

Friendship

Tolly

One night, I snuck out of my house to meet up with my friends. I was dressed in a black tracksuit with my braids in the colour 1B and styled in my signature hairstyle – the pick and drop. We weren't meeting up to go to a party, nor were we off to meet boys. We were out to seek revenge. Revenge on a guy who had hurt my friend. Earlier that day we had found out that this guy, who my friend was pregnant by, was seeing another girl. We were around sixteen and seventeen at the time and this guy was twenty-one. What had started as some sort of fantasy where we all rolled up to his house to egg it and drape it with tissue had become a reality. We were ready to ride.

Armed with eggs and cheap toilet rolls, we stood outside his house. On the count of three, we started throwing them and shouting out swear words in-between our laughs. In the midst of our revenge mission, the guy came outside and chased us down the road with a baseball bat. We all separated and ran away, screaming but still laughing. I found a car to hide under and I laid flat, face down on the floor, for what felt like hours. This sounds like a scene that could have been slotted into a bad British remake of *Set It Off*, but to me, it's one of my greatest examples of friendship. It was Black girls being there for each other – it was sisterhood. My friend found solace and, I guess, strength in us, and I know I shouldn't be making a bunch of teenage girls egging a house sound poetic, but honestly, it was beautiful.

✧

This idea of riding out is one I've taken into all of my friendships. My friends are crucial to who I am. My friends are my soulmates; they feed me. Being a friend is a role I take very seriously. So, under the guise of 'I'm writing a book', I asked four of my closest friends what kind of friend they thought I was. This was partly indulgent but also very important to me. I needed to see if I give them what they give to me.

> My friends are my soulmates; they feed me.

My oldest friend said, 'Friend? I think you have the wrong person, you're my sister.' Which, of course, made me tear up. She continued with, 'Well, for me, I think you're a friend that creates a safe space. A place where I'm comfortable enough to be very honest with myself. You're also my fun friend so you help with what could be a boring life, and you're the friend that's always honest with me.'

My best boy friend decided to not reply in fully formed sentences and just sent me some words, because men.

The words read: 'Good friend. Helpful. A good listener. A pagan at times. You have a good heart.'

My best friend replied saying, 'You're the person I'm calling when it's time to make a tough decision. You're the person I'm calling to laugh from the depths of my soul. You're the person I'm calling when it's time to cause mischief. When the tears are already flowing. When I just need someone that feels like home. You're a whole complete sanctuary, Tolani. And you're that sanctuary for so many of your loved ones, so gracefully. You're smart. You see the world in stories and insights. You're fiercely loyal. You're ambitious. You'll call your people out, with love. You know life is for the living. I've seen you move through life with unmatched integrity for over ten years, my friend.'

And one of my favourite people in the world said: 'You are the embodiment of empathy. You care for your friends more than you care for yourself and you always remind me to take care of myself even when you're not around.'

I love how much my friends love me; it shapes my whole world.

Being around Black women and being loved by them is a form of freedom for me.

I cannot write about friendship without talking about my friendships with Black women. Being around Black women and being loved by them is a form of freedom for me. I do not have to hide any part of who I am. It's the way we laugh loudly, regardless of where the fuck we are. It's how we compliment each other, and it's the shared joy we have when Drake's 'Nice for What' comes on. It's the fact that they share my experiences; they know what it feels like to manoeuvre around this world in the Black female body. If anyone is capable of great friendship, it is a Black woman; a statement I make based on a lifetime of observation.

You see, I am good at friendships, I could be a better friend at times, but I am a good friend. I follow the rules of Girl Code and I have even made up a version of my own – what I like to call 'boundaries'. Some of the rules are exclusive to my close friends – if you are an acquaintance, I will date your ex – while some rules apply to all. I have found that in order to preserve friendships, these boundaries need to be considered. I take this code seriously.

My first fight, in the name of friendship, happened because the Girl Code was broken. My best friend at the time was going out with a guy, and the relationship was as serious as all relationships are when you are fourteen. She had been unwell so was not in school for a few days. During those few days, it came out that her boyfriend had kissed another girl at the back of the fields. An important detail, because all the sinful things we got up to happened at the back of the fields. The girl he kissed was our friend, albeit not a close friend, but she was a friend. So, of course, I took this betrayal personally and decided to fight this girl. Even though my best friend and this girl made up (and, according to Facebook, are still friends to this day), I was unable to forgive her because the trust had been broken. And yes, looking at the situation through adult eyes, my best friend's boyfriend should have got all the blame. Of course this girl wanted to lips him: he was one of the best-looking guys in our year; blonde, blue-eyed and, unlike the other uncultured swines, he used wax instead of gel to style his hair. However, I still maintain that this breaking of Girl Code was not acceptable. The thing is, girl codes protect friendships and I am not saying that everyone should be governed by them but, in order for any friendship to work, some of the codes can't be negotiated. Anyone who has been friends with anyone knows that there are some things loyal friends just don't do.

In case you haven't noticed, I am a girl's girl. I don't trust women who brag about not getting on with other women. With that being said, my friendships with men also mean the world to me. Platonic relationships are always under some sort of questioning; they're either seen as a version of unrequited love or a friend-with-benefits type situation. There have been people much smarter than me who have conducted psychological studies to prove whether men and women can just be friends. One study conducted in 2012 by April Bleske-Rechek et al. (hold tight, my Research Methods module at university becoming useful) concluded that men and women can't be friends because men just want to beat.* I mean, they broke it down in better terms,

* April L. Bleske and David M. Buss, 'Can men and women be just friends?', *Personal Relationships* (2000).

but ultimately, they were saying that platonic friendships all have sexual impulses under the surface. However a 2014 study by Carlin Flora found that men and women can just be friends. She says 'given the importance of social support to a healthy mind and body, it is unwise to kick half of the population out of your pool of potential friends' and I am inclined to side with Flora.* My friendships with men have an absence of physical attraction, sex and passion, but they are loaded with affection and care. If I am totally honest, I depend on these friendships to see the good in men. These platonic friendships give me consistency and stability – two things I have not felt in romantic relationships.

And although there is a lack of attraction, my friendships with guys don't depend on my being one of the boys, in fact, I make it apparent that I am not one of the boys. I am not a 'cool girl'. I am none of the things Gillian Flynn talks about in *Gone Girl*. Yes, I am hot, brilliant and funny but I do not adore football. In fact, I hate it and I have no desire to know what the offside rule is. I've never played poker and I only find *some* dirty jokes funny. I think burping loudly is nasty and I don't play video games. No amount of thirst will ever make me drink cheap beer. I don't particularly want a threesome and anal sex feels like something that should just happen on birthdays and special occasions. I would like to think I eat hot dogs and hamburgers with class and I am certainly not a size two. I am far from a cool girl; I am very much a girly girl. My rules for my friendships

---

* Carlin Flora, 'Just Friends', *Scentific American Mind* (2014).

with guys are that my version of femininity is not up for questioning and that they do not lay claim on my body. Because, even in friendship, men want to make sure you're not sleeping around.

What's apparent to me, in friendships with both men and women is that, contrary to what the Spice Girls said, friendships do end. And when they end, it hurts. A lot. I have had a few friendship break-ups and most of them just dissolved over time. I never had a fight with my best friend from primary school, we just went to different secondary schools and, after a summer of trying to make the friendship work, we separated. The same happened with my best friends from secondary school and many of my friends over my lifetime – we just grew apart. But the break-ups that hurt the most were the ones I had to end; the ones when the friendship stopped feeling good.

I always know when it's time to end a friendship. I'm big on being around people who bring out the best in me. People who I feel good around. My friends protect me, nurture me and uplift me. I feel safe with them. If this is no longer true with a friend, then I start to question the friendship. My friendships are grounded in authenticity so if we are unable to be our true selves around each other, we shouldn't be friends. These conversations are hard and I have often avoided them. I have done the childish thing of just not replying to messages and not calling back. I regret this and it took someone doing it to me to make me see how unkind it is. There's something a little evil in not giving someone closure, not letting them know what they have done to you and leaving them in a state of questioning.

The break-up that I still find difficult to forgive myself for is one that ended in an argument centred around a man – a man who I had no problem consistently forgiving for all his wrongdoings. I had asked her to stop talking to the said guy because their relationship made me uncomfortable and he was a man that had hurt me, a hurt she knew about and had comforted me through. Her being his friend felt like she was choosing him over me and I couldn't forgive that. I tend to be less forgiving of friends because I expect better from them and I don't think I am alone in this. I have seen women refuse to leave partners who have cheated on them and hurt them, but a friend does one thing wrong and they call it quits. After several weeks of ignoring her calls and messages I decided to tell her the friendship was over. This conversation is one no one preps you for, in fact as an adult saying, 'I don't want to be friends with you any more' feels childish. The conversation was hard. Ending things with someone who had been part of so many of my punctuation mark moments was painful. It's different to the end of romantic relationships, that comes with rules that we all know about, this pain was new. I still think about her at times. So many of my throwback pictures have her in them, yet I am aware it's too far gone. I refused all her attempts to keep in contact and never accepted her apologies.

Obviously there's a huge difference between friendships and romantic relationships because expectations are different.

Romantic relationships unlock new levels. You're talking, you're seeing each other, you're dating, you're official, you're engaged and then you're married. I am exhausted just writing that, let alone going through it. What I am trying to say is that romantic relationships go through all these stages and each stage comes with its own expectations that are communicated. Friendships just tend to jump from friend to close friend and then maybe to best friend. The thing is, I think friendships should follow the lead of romantic relationships. OK, we don't have to add a title to each stage, but we should keep communicating our expectations. We should express our needs and set our boundaries. Friendships should feel like that beautiful and uplifting Jack Johnson song, you know, the one that goes:

It's always better when we're together.

It fills you with great memories and leaves you looking forward to making new ones.

✧

Audrey

We talk a lot about friendships on the podcast and it's for a reason. My friendships are some of the most important relationships in my life because they're an extension of me. When I think about all the friends I've had in my life, past and present, the one common denominator is that they're all like me. We like the same things, have similar upbringings, we enjoy the finer things in life and have similar hopes and dreams for the future. Even my many imaginary friends were like me – shout out Alina and Sophie, they were real ones. I've always had the ability to make friends quite easily as far back as primary school. I remember walking into reception and, after scoping out my crush of course, I approached a girl with the biggest green eyes and a fringe so long you could barely see them and said, 'Do you want to be friends?' Even at the age of four, I was *that* bold.

My role in all my friendship groups over the years has been the funny friend, the silly one who tells the corny jokes. I'm also the friend who's down to go to the club because your crush is going to be there. The friend who'll send you a voice note saying 'OMG guess who I just saw . . .' I've been described as an enabler on a few occasions because I have a tendency to egg on my friend's impulsive decisions, especially when it comes to men, but it's all in fun, I promise. I'm that friend you can call and say you want to text your crush, even though you know you shouldn't, and I'll reply with a well written response for you to send to them. I want my friends to feel like they can talk to me about anything and not feel judged. It's so important that my friends understand there's nothing

> I'm that friend you can call and say you want to text your crush, even though you know you shouldn't, and I'll reply with a well written response for you to send to them.

they can tell me that will make me see them in a different light (within reason) and I pride myself on allowing my friends to be their full selves around me. In fact, if you're going to be my friend, it's imperative because, for me, it shows a lack of trust if you can't be your free and true self.

My mum taught me many lessons about friendships, some I agree with and some I don't, but as I've gotten older I've realised that, as wise, smart and amazing as my mum is, our life experiences have been so different that her advice doesn't always translate to my life. However, one thing she's never gotten wrong is her ability to sense the wrong'uns that I've introduced her to. *Every* mum has this sixth sense. A friend can walk in the door, be as polite as anything with the best manners and as soon as they leave, your mum will look at you knowingly and say, 'Be careful with that one.' This happened on so many occasions with my friends and I remember I'd get so defensive and annoyed but looking back, she was never ever wrong. I hope I have that sixth sense with my future children. Growing up, I remember hearing whispers and conversations between my parents about certain friends of theirs, aunties and uncles who were here today and gone tomorrow, and I think this has definitely influenced the way my mum educated me on friends. My mum swears blind that I can't trust anyone except for her and that my problems aren't to be shared, but again, it took me a while to understand that her strong African upbringing differs so much from my westernised experiences, so I pick and choose what I agree with and this isn't one of them. My friends have been instrumental in me having a place of healing and I've shared some of my deepest darkest secrets with them and feel much better for it.

I'm someone who knows a lot of people and one thing I had to learn (which I didn't action until I was well into my thirties) was being able to separate people into categories. Some may have described me as 'bait' (someone who's known or popular) and even though on paper that doesn't sound like a bad thing, there are some negative connotations that come with it. Nevertheless, I decided to take ownership of this and make it a positive. I went to a popular university and worked in Selfridges and everyone knows if you could get a job there, you were *lit*. This meant I met a lot of people, and that, coupled with the fact that

I've always maintained friendships and haven't changed my number since 2007, means I've kept in contact with *a lot* of people. Being this bait on top of doing the podcast means I've been exposed to a lot more people than the average person. Initially, I struggled to categorise people and ended up referring to everyone as a friend. I eventually learned that not everyone should hold this title and it's OK to be able to distinguish between your friends, acquaintances and people you just know. Part of why I feel this is important is because everyone can't hold the same weight – how could I put people who know everything about me, have been to my parents' house and were at my wedding on the same level as people whose last names I don't even know?

As someone who's had friendships that span as long as twenty years, one thing I'm constantly learning is how to navigate a friendship when your life journeys aren't on the same trajectory. Sometimes it takes work to find common ground and when you can no longer find this, you might have to let that friend go – that's where the phrase 'seasons and reasons' comes into play. There have been friendships I've had which have broken down naturally without any big arguments – we've just grown apart. There have been others where I could feel us drifting so I worked extra hard to fight for that friendship. There are the friends who you don't speak to every day but when you get together, it's as if nothing has changed; even though this is such a blessing, I think it's important not to take these friendships for granted. You still need to nurture them and this is something I try really hard to do, even to the detriment of other things in my life, including my marriage. I've always struggled saying no and I'm still a work in progress.

Friendship fall-outs are inevitable and I've seen a lot of my friendships fade to black but there have been very few where I've had to cut someone off. I have a very tolerant personality, so it takes a lot for me to get to that place with someone but there's one scenario that stands out to me where I came to the end of my tolerance. She was a friend I grew up with, let's call her Florence, and she had a very troubled upbringing. I think this was one of the reasons why I let her get away with so much. She did so many unforgivable things to me but I always chalked it up to her not knowing any better. Shit hit the fan when she spread a horrible rumour that I was being sexually abused by a family member to everyone on my estate. It was a complete lie and she did it in retaliation to me telling her that I could no longer be friends with her after a series of incidents that had built up – the final straw being when she stole a ring from my grandmother's house.

It was difficult because I was young and naïve; I'd never cut anyone off before and she lived close to me so I had to see her every day and make a conscious effort not to talk to her. Eventually she moved away, and I wasn't to see her for another eight years. This whole situation was incredibly difficult for a number of reasons, one huge one being the guilt of cutting someone off who already had it so hard. It was also tough because when she wasn't snaking me I actually loved her; it was almost like a mild form of

Stockholm syndrome. I'd hang on to the good memories through every bad situation but I learned that I couldn't let guilt make me stay to the detriment of my own happiness and peace of mind. Even though I wanted to end the friendship, it was still painful. One thing was clear though: sometimes you have to cut out the disease before it spreads because no one should be able to get away with abusing your kindness.

Even though I've had a few bad experiences, I've mostly been lucky in my friendships where each of them offer me a safe non-judgmental space where I can vent, no matter how big or small my worries are. That being said, I know I'm far from perfect. I've made some poor decisions when it comes to choosing friends at times, mainly because I'm such an open book and have never subscribed to the no new friends rule. In fact, I think I've taken it to the extreme opposite end of the spectrum and, at times, have made myself too open and available to people who aren't necessarily deserving of such a privilege. When I say 'privilege', I mean it a non-arrogant way, I promise, but everyone should value themselves in this regard. You can't let any old person access that much of your humanity – you need to protect yourself as much as you can and feel people out first. A way of doing this, I have realised, is seeing how they treat the friends that were there before you – it can be eye-opening.

Sharing friends is always something I've prided myself on – remember how I said all my friends are like me? This has meant that a lot of my friendship groups have merged and I honestly love it so much. I know a lot of people feel weird about this concept and I totally understand because it can become messy and political, with people often very territorial over their friends. So am I, but so far so good. I love that I can have a drama-free birthday dinner with all my girls. I'm like a proud mamma watching everyone bond, maybe there's an element of ego to it. My hen-do in Las Vegas was the biggest testament to this, where I invited twenty of my closest friends and never thought anything of it because I knew they would all get along. I think the reason I've been able to channel this is because I apply the same approach to all my relationships – finding a balance between being territorial while allowing people the freedom to be themselves. I want anyone in my life to be there because they want to be, the same way I want people to support the podcast because they want to, not because they feel obligated. I feel so confident in what I bring to my friendships that the idea of my friends being close outside of me isn't a threat; I think people fear being replaced which is why they keep things close to their chest. Kelechi Okafor often says on her podcast *Say Your Mind* that you block your own blessings if you work from a place of scarcity; blessings will never run out so there is *no need*. I guess what I'm saying is that sharing friends doesn't taint what I have with each person and if it does, it means the friendship wasn't strong enough to begin with. *However,* you man aren't allowed to go out without inviting me . . .

✧

Audrey

Now, it wouldn't be a friendship chapter without giving some of these women an honorable mention:

My best friend, Rachael, knows everything about me. We have such a unique bond because we're so similar and people have asked if we're sisters because we're so in sync. We met in 2004 when we both worked in Selfridges and pretty much hit it off straight away. She took me under her wing when I moved to the Menswear section and really, Rach and I have been through it *all*. That's my rider right there. She taught me how to dress because, Lord knows, I was a mess, hunny. We've had the best holidays, baecations and just life moments together, with some of the funniest stories which we'll take to the grave. I'll never forget when I was seeing a guy and we hacked his emails to find out that I was a side chick, or when we got wasted in Miami and I got taken out on a stretcher, or the all-nighters where we'd rave then go straight to work the next day. The most magical thing about our friendship is the fact our lives have been pretty parallel and, even when we've nearly gone off track, we've found a way to pull it back. We both value our friendship and because of that, I think we'll forever be solid. Most importantly she's also not afraid to tell me about myself, which we *all* need in our lives.

The women who I chose to be my bridesmaids: Rachael, Kirsten, Mahalia, Nadia and, of course, my sister Vanessa, have all contributed massively to the woman I am today, which is exactly why I chose them. Supportive and honest friends can be hard to come by and each of these women have played a significant role in my life throughout our friendships. Whether it's been bailing me out of situations financially, picking me up when I've been stranded or giving me the real when I'm in the wrong, these are the women that know Audrey, not 'Ghana's Finest'. I have a very different relationship with each person but that's the magic. I call them my A1s from day 1 because that's exactly what they are. I met Nadia at university in 2004, after people around campus would randomly say to me, 'Have you met Nadia? I think you guys would really get along.' When we did, they couldn't have been more right. After more than fifteen years of friendship, I've never seen Nadia in a bad mood or in bad spirits, her personality is contagious and she's just good vibes all around.

Kirsten is who I call my honorary Ghanaian cousin and, funnily enough, our dads were friends in Ghana *way before* we were even born. Kirsten is loyal as fuck and I can always rely on her to give it to me as real they come. She will also take a secret to the grave and beyond. Mahalia, aka My M's, has a heart of gold. We went to sixth form together and, while we weren't actually friends then, we later formed a friendship through my husband Nick and became super close. Mahalia is an empath who literally feels what you feel, so if I'm sad, she's sad. We also share a deep bond over our love for *Real Housewives* and food.

My sister Vanessa, the love of my life, I'll get to you later!

These women have showered me with love and when the podcast became successful, they never stopped supporting it. They continuously celebrate my wins even when I don't, and nothing is done out of obligation, but out of love. When I got married, I couldn't afford to get them brides-maids gifts or pay for their dresses, but that didn't matter to them. They showed up and showed out for me, making my hen the best holiday of my life. This is why they all had to be in my first book.

✧

What are the rules when it comes to friendships? The truth is, I don't have all the answers but what I do know is that some friendships will fade away and naturally come to an end, whereas others will stick with you for life.

I received a DM once from a young girl who asked, 'How do you have so many friends and how do I make friends?' It's a fair question and, while I do consider myself to be so blessed to have loads of amazing friends, there's no secret to it, plus, you also don't need to have loads of friends if that isn't who you are. It's important to remember it's quality over quantity, keeping up with loads of people can even be hard work sometimes. If bringing your friendship circles together is practical and can work, I would say do it as it saves a lot of time when you're planning birthday celebrations!

Don't forget that friendships are no different to relation-ships and, for them to be successful, you have to nurture them. Don't always wait to check in, but if you're always the friend checking in, then let that be known. If you're the busy friend, then try and make time – we're so lucky with all the technology we have that there's really no excuse. Making new friends seems so tough the older you get but make yourself open to it. If you value your friends, show them. Let them know you love them in whatever way that looks like. Hold them accountable and allow them to hold you accountable without seeing it as a negative but rather, a form of growth. Check on your strong friends and remember that you chose this relationship, so enjoy it to its fullest capacity.

Milena

I don't know about anyone else but with my friendships, it's almost like I'm in a relationship. I need to know if they got home alright, what their plans are for the day, how their day at work was and they best know that if I'm calling or messaging them at one o'clock in the morning, I'm expecting a quick answer. Because of this, friendships are very important to me. In fact, I think they are the most important kind of 'ship'. I don't think I could cope with life without their support and, if we're honest, their lives wouldn't be great without me – I'd definitely be missed. The late-night conversations, the holding my hair back while I'm being sick, the co-writing of text messages for my ex, the singing at the top of our lungs to those 'I don't need no man' type of tunes, I'd love to re-live all of it. To be honest, I think all of my friends are sick of my shit – nothing shocks them when it comes to me any more. I could literally walk into the room naked and they would be so blasé about it. One thing is for certain though: there is never a dull moment with us and when I say we laugh with each other, we *laugh*. Every single one of my friends is hilarious and humour is how we get through life.

If we're working with the analogy that friendships are like relationships, then we have to accept that there are going to be negatives as well as positives, and like with romantic love, I learned the hard way. The expectations I have for my friendships are very basic: we need to be there for each other, be truthful with each other, uplift each other and be able to be our authentic selves around one another. Upon reflection, there have been some situations I wish I could have handled differently but I think acknowledging and taking accountability is the tough beauty of growth. I've had a history of holding onto friendships that were of no benefit to me and forgiving 'friends' for constantly letting me down or leaving me out. I could never pinpoint why it was that I just couldn't let these individuals go because I knew they were bad friends that didn't hold me in the same regard I held them in. Much like my relationships, my friendships highlighted my attachment issues which stemmed from my childhood and that feeling of abandonment I always had. I used to be quite territorial over the people in my life so when I saw my friends get new friends, I would feel a bit of a way because I was scared that they would forget about me (can I just say sorry to my friends again for this – I know it wasn't easy dealing with my shit, love you). I've since learned to confront these issues within

> There have been some situations I wish I could have handled differently but I think acknowledging and taking accountability is the tough beauty of growth.

myself and realised that this wasn't a healthy attachment to project onto other people, so I totally understand friends feeling overwhelmed with it all. Thankfully, I've worked on myself now.

✧

There are different types of friendships most of us can relate to having. I'm pretty sure we all have that one family member that is like our best friend and for me, that's my cousin Natasha. We've always said that the title of being cousins doesn't actually depict just how close we are because she is practically my sister. Having grown up together we have so many memories that I will never forget. One of my favourite ones was when we went on a double date and she didn't like the guy she was with. Instead of just making up excuses, she faked passing out and I told them both to go and get help so we could run away by the time they got back. We think about that day often. We definitely know each other inside and out – almost quite literally because our WhatsApp media consists of pictures of all our body parts like a doctor's surgery inbox! This woman has calmed me on so many different occasions; she's helped me through my anxiety break downs and coached me through my panic attacks. We were also pregnant at the same time and it's *so* special to have our kids growing up with that bond that we had. She has asked me to be the maid of honour at her wedding and I honestly feel so blessed to have someone like her in my life. This is the type of friendship you know you will have forever.

Friendship

I'm lucky enough to have two family members that are like best friends and the second is my cousin is Jeni, and although the North Atlantic Ocean separates us thanks to her living in the US, we are incredibly close. I remember the first time she came to visit: we were identical – even down to the pizza we loved to eat. It was as if I had a doppelgänger living on the other side of the world. Despite the distance, she came back three times between 2013 and 2019. It was so tough saying goodbye after having her for two weeks but the memories that we have created have been so beautiful, and though I missed her wedding (fuck you, COVID-19), I was able to be there via FaceTime. At the end of 2019, *The Receipts Podcast* had a UK tour, I told Jeni about it and next thing I knew, I had a text saying 'BITCH I AM COMING TO LONDON' with her flight tickets attached for November – just so that she could come to one of our shows, I couldn't believe it. Having her watch me on stage and travelling with me was the best thing ever, we had so much fun and I was so grateful to just be together. I cannot wait to take my ass to America so we can laugh again.

Then you need your go-to friends and for me, these are Alice, Shannon, Anita and Mandy. These are the people that can tell you how it is without you wanting to punch them up, put you in your place at times when you need a reality check and will stay up with you until four in the morning, talking about the shit going on in each other's lives without it feeling like a burden. Alice, Shannon, Anita and Mandy all have unique qualities that I love, and

I have amazing memories with them that I will forever cherish. I'd like to share some of these with you because it's my essay and why not?

Firstly, there is Alice. I will never forget how she has been there for me on multiple occasions, but specifically there for me when I was at my lowest during my pregnancy. I was definitely never short of that tough love with her, but she knew how to give it to me because she loved me and wanted me to see sense and, for that, I am so grateful! Al and I call each other 'Beavs' (short for beavers). Let me explain: when we were younger, we had a sleepover and decided to prank call strip-clubs asking for auditions and we would hang up in stitches. There was one club that I called and asked if it was OK that 'I had a hairy beaver'. I locked off and we were rolling around on the floor in *tears*. From that day on, the name stuck. In every birthday card, Christmas card, social media post and texts, we refer to one another as beavs and that will never change. I applaud the fact that she has such a beautiful family and has been able to build a stable environment for her two boys with her husband and, though she's a little younger than me, she is like a motherly figure to me that I can go to for everything and anything.

Then there's Shannon, who is probably my most protective, caring and loyal friend. She is that one person who would go along with anything. She might be a little reluctant but would still follow my madness, no matter how much money is in our bank accounts! Our go-to was always Mother Bar in Shoreditch and we went there so often that we even knew some of the bouncers on a first-name basis. Sometimes, we would even get let in for free and if anyone tried it with us, we could have gotten them kicked out. Our daughters are best friends and it's so beautiful to see our Mini Mes love each other the way we love one another. I'm more affectionate than Shan but, over time, I've learned that just because I love all the kisses and hugs and she doesn't it doesn't mean she loves me any less – she shows me her love by being a ride or die.

Then there's my good friend Anita. We used to go to school together but, for the last couple of years, we have really bonded over glasses of wine and girly chats at her house. To this day, I can't forget the fact that she had the cheek to give me tea in a glass mug and say that it was a normal thing to do. I *strongly* disagree. This girl is like my personal therapist – there isn't anything I couldn't talk to her about and I always feel like I'm in a non-judgement zone with her. She brings me down to earth and helps me rationalise a lot of my thoughts. The ability she has to put things into perspective is beautiful! I also admire Anita's strength, she's faced some difficult things but she still manages to carry on in life so gracefully, I just love her soul. She is a gentle breeze that goes into hiding some-times, but she knows her friends will always understand that it's not personal. The love stays strong through these periods.

Last but not least, is my oldest friend Mandy. I've known her for twenty-five years. We met in nursery and were best friends. She's the friend that you don't see or speak to every day but when you do meet up, it's like *nothing* has changed. This woman made a plan with what she wanted in life and she executed it – it's so beautiful to see. I am so proud of everything she has achieved and we can't wait to recreate all the pictures and music videos we have from our childhood with our daughters.

I also have a friendship that seems to be quite rare and is one that not very many people understand, and that's the friendship I have with my baby father. We live in a world where some people are mad enough to even think that men and women who have kids together cannot be 'just friends', so you can imagine the uproar caused by me and my baby dad being close. I'm not even going to lie and say that it wasn't a difficult process to get to where I am now with this man and there is still further to go. When we broke up, I was really hurt that I wasn't able to make my little family work the way I wanted to. For a while, I wasn't able to switch off that feeling of hurt, but we were always civil and we wanted to be on good terms because of all our history. This was easier said than done. After some time, when the pain of the break-up started to fade and we both began to properly move on with life, it was almost as if someone pressed a refresh button and we became the close friends we always knew we could be. Though for the most part we are cool and we get on, there are phases the friendship goes through where things stale or struggle, but that's the reality of it and I like the balance.

We never really had issues establishing our friendship because it had always been there, which was one of the reasons we lasted so long as a couple in the first place. We just had to learn that we could not overstep certain boundaries or be overly intrusive in each other's lives and decisions. Although sometimes I was, and OK, I am a bit extra, but so what? At the start, I constantly needed to remember that we were no longer together and I could not try to dictate things – like his love life – as it wasn't my place to say anything any more, or so he thought (joking). It was definitely hard to differentiate our new relationship as friends when I had been his girlfriend for almost nine years, but after trial and error, we have managed to get to a very positive stage in our relationship for the sake of our daughter. Our friendship was definitely misunderstood and judged by practically everyone around us. Nobody could comprehend how we could become such close friends after having been together for so long and breaking up. Everybody assumes that just because we are stuck in each other's lives forever, this comes with a sense of entitlement to sex, but I can assure any side chick of his that this isn't the case. It's so funny to me that people would rather normalise parents that hate each other rather than parents that get along and have a platonic relationship! In my head, it's simple: we got together when we were teenagers, we eventually grew out of our relationship and began to realise that, although we had love *for* each other, we were no longer *in* love with each other. I can understand how our relationship would have been a hard pill for many to swallow but I'm glad my baby father and I were able to put aside any issues for the sake of Cataleya.

Anyways, I could be here all day talking about all the memories I have with everybody – there are too many to think about. What I've learned over time is that friendship requires as much effort, commitment and love as any other relationship. It won't always be smooth sailing and you may not always be friends with someone forever but that is OK, we're only human and changes happen. I'm a strong believer in putting yourself out there because you never know what could come from it and so making friends has never really been an issue for me. In fact, I even tend to overshare a bit the first time I meet someone just for the sake of creating conversation and making them feel a bit more comfortable with me, which I later tend to look back at and think 'wtf Milena'. This led to me using the term 'friend' quite loosely because my overly-attached ass got a bit too excited after having a handful of conversations with someone; guys, just save yourself the embarrassment and learn from me please and thanks. Other than that, my main advice to you reading this is to really appreciate your friends and be there for each other, as you never know what someone is going through behind closed doors, especially during these times when it feels most people are judgmental and harsh. Don't forget to celebrate their wins, no matter how small you may think they are! Having people to lean back on is a necessity. Finally, communicate and talk about your feelings, actually listen to and consider what they say, don't just reply with whatever it is you want to say. At the end of the day, where would we be without our friends, ey?

✧

Audrey's Jokes

What would this book be without some jokes curated by comedy queen and Ghana's finest, Audrey?

Audrey's Jokes

How does Moses like his coffee?

Hebrews it.

What did the location wear to the party?

A dress.

How much does a chimney cost?

Nothing, it's on the house.

What do *The Sixth Sense* and the *Titanic* have in common?

Icy dead people.

Why don't eggs tell each other jokes?

They might crack themselves up.

Did you hear the rumour about butter?

Well, I'm not going to spread it.

What does cheese say when it looks in the mirror?

Halloumi.

A duck walks into a bar and he says to the landlord, 'Do you have any bread?'

The landlord replies, 'We don't sell bread.'

The next day the duck comes back again and says, 'Do you have any bread?'

And the landlord replies, 'We don't sell bread.'

The next day the duck comes back again and says, 'Do you have any bread?'

The landlord says, 'Listen here, Duck, we don't sell bread and if you come back here and ask me that again I'm going to nail your beak down to the bar.'

The next day the duck comes back again and says, 'Do you have any nails?'

And the landlord says, 'Why in the hell would I have nails?'

The duck replies, 'Well have you got any bread then?'

Tolly

I had always thought that sex was for men, something that was solely created for their pleasure. It would explain why they gagged for it so much, why sex was consistently sold and bought by them, why they found the sight of boobs – literally bags of fat drooping from a woman's chest – so alluring and distracting. Sex had to be for them. Women rarely spoke about it the way men did, in fact, from what I heard, women mainly used sex as a bargaining tool; it was a way to get what they really wanted. Aunties used it as a way to reward or punish their partners while the girls at school used sex in exchange for love and attention. The notion of women getting pleasure from sex never really came up.

Sex was never really spoken about in conversations that were for me. Yes, I overheard my mum and aunties talk about it, but around me and my sisters, my mum never even said the word sex. She called it 'fun', but the term was laden with shame and fear. This 'fun' was not only going to 'cheapen you', it was also going to get you pregnant, which, of course, would bring shame on the family. The only version of 'the talk' I had was after I started my period. My mum sat me down on the bed and said that I should not let boys near me because I would get pregnant. And then there was church, where the youth leaders further cemented the idea that sex, my body and my sex parts were bad and that I was to be a good girl. So, on the day that I watched Usher on *Top of the Pops* and I felt the twinge of my fanny fluttering, I ran upstairs to rinse it because I felt shame. Whenever I would sneak a look at the 'Position of the Week' in *More!* magazine or I just happened to watch *Eurotrash*, I felt shame. I was made to believe that I had no business enjoying sex and felt disgusted with my body when it was turned on without my approval. My sexuality never really belonged to me, and nor did I try to claim it.

> I was made to believe that I had no business enjoying sex and felt disgusted with my body when it was turned on without my approval.

From a young age, I knew that my body was up for consumption and it was up to me to keep it safe. Keeping it safe meant avoiding sex and making sure my body didn't exude sexiness. I was told to close my legs, sit like a lady, and not wear clothes that were too short or too tight because it would attract men. This wasn't just something I was just told at home and in church; my social circles said the same. My sexuality was policed everywhere I went. I have a clear memory of sucking on a lollipop – a strawberry and cream Chupa Chups, to be exact – and a guy, who was older, telling me to just keep the lollipop in my mouth. I was thirteen and he was fifteen and we were standing outside the gates of secondary school when he said taking it in and out would make it look like I suck dick and I shouldn't let anyone know that I suck dick. I assume he would be very disappointed if he was to ever find out the amount of pleasure I now get from sucking dick.

Even with all of this in mind, I lost my virginity at a young age. I guess my want for love and approval quieted my shame. I was having sex because it was what you were meant to do with your boyfriend; it had very little to do with what I wanted or whether I was ready. I was doing it for him so it was fine. I didn't even consider my need or want for pleasure because I was there to please. I like to be of service so this suited me just fine.

My first time was completely unlike my expectations or anything I had watched in American teenage movies. There wasn't a rose petal in sight nor did it have an R&B soundtrack. In fact, it was soundtracked to the moans of my discomfort and Twista's 'Slow Jamz', featuring Kanye West and Jamie Foxx. If memory serves me right, the sex finished before the song did. Once it was done, we attempted to flush the purple-coloured condom but, after several failed attempts, the condom was fished out of the toilet bowl and wrapped in toilet roll before it was thrown in the bin. And that was it – that was my first time.

Sex

My world was not set alight and I felt awful afterwards. It cemented my theory that sex was for men. I carried on only having sex with this one person and my sex life became a series of thrusting in different positions. My measurement of good sex was dependent on his reaction and my ability to make him come; I never experienced my own orgasm. I saw myself as a sexualised commodity, with my sexuality only existing to turn on my boyfriend. So while I decided I didn't like sex, I found that I did like the label of being sexually giving; I liked having the power and means to sexually please someone. Sex was never about me. I had sex because I loved my boyfriend and when that relationship ended, I was glad that went with it. I no longer had fake orgasms to soothe his ego or had to have my body used for masturbation. I was happy to have my body back and have it safe, after years of using it as a tool.

✧

Everything you read about break-ups and heartbreak is hinged on feelings and emotions, but a lot of the healing that took place after my break-up was linked with my body. It sparked my decision to not have sex any more, with anyone. I no longer needed to do it as an act of love so therefore I no longer needed to do it at all. As a Christian, people assume my decision to not have sex was based on religion, but it wasn't – sorry, God. I just never wanted to feel the aftermath of sex again. I never felt that release of dopamine or serotonin like the experts promise. I just felt like shit, like I had been used. And if I felt this bad after having sex with someone I loved, how would I feel doing it with someone who didn't have to text me back? This fear, or anxiety, stopped me from ever wanting to have sex.

However, outside of my sexless world, conversations around sex were changing. My friends had started having good sex and were exchanging stories of orgasms and knee shakes. *The Receipts Podcast* started and I was around women who were normalising conversations around female pleasure. We were having conversations that didn't include feeling shame for our sexual needs, feelings and experiences. These conversations made me wonder if something was wrong with me because, unlike other single girls who were having casual sex, I was unable to open myself up to being turned on by the men I was dating. Sex with these men didn't feel safe, and

> *The Receipts Podcast started and I was around women who were normalising conversations around female pleasure.*

though I did not feel they were going to hurt me, I still didn't want to share my body with them. But my want to be desired had not stopped, and in the end, I met a man. A man I wanted to have sex with, but still, my fear of the aftermath would override my arousal.

It was this that made me realise that I had to define what sex was for me and what it meant to me, outside of my friends' realities. Casual sex, by its definition, was something I quickly ruled out. Now, this doesn't mean that I am against it, but I believe that sexual freedom must also include the freedom to not have casual sex, or any sex at all. Sex for me has to come with trust and emotions and I can only consider it if I feel an emotional connection with that person. This emotional connection is not under any constraints of time – I just need to feel something for them. This is a sentiment that not everyone shares and I often feel prudish when hearing that women are able to have sex with just anyone. When I have explained to people my feelings and sexual history, they have told me to just get back on the horse, and by horse, they meant dick, but getting autonomy over my body goes beyond that. I have had to unlearn all the teachings I had around sex, from my home and from church. It took me a long time to accept the idea of being a sexual being: admitting that I wanted to have sex with men I felt a connection with and to give myself permission and freedom to feel pleasure. My pussy is mine – it is not a tool for the person who is currently penetrating it. It is mine and I needed to take ownership of it.

You see, me and my body had issues. These issues ran deeper than my dislike for my belly bulging over my jeans or that bit of fat between the armpit and chest which no one really has a use for. In fact, my body issues never centred around its image. I liked its image: the way it allowed clothes to cling on to it, the slight drop of my breasts and the way my nipples need to show up even when they're not invited. I understood why men liked it and I had used it as a tool to please a man for years. My issue with my body was that I never allowed it to feel pleasure, I would sometimes feel myself stiffen up when my body even hinted it wanted sexual pleasure. I learned to numb feelings and thoughts of desire because of the shame I had associated with it. I wanted to change this. I wanted to experience bliss and allow my body to sink into its own pleasures, and the safest option to do that was masturbation.

Just like sex, masturbation also came with shame for me. Rather than seeing masturbation as a form of self-care and getting to know my body, I thought it weird and, again, pictured an uncomfortable aftermath. The story of how I started masturbating is an interesting one. A sex toy was sent to my house after a conversation with a man who promised to do anything to make sure I experienced sexual pleasure. The significance of a man being the one who did this for me is not lost on me. After years of feeling like sex was just men taking something from me, I felt there was something precious about a man wanting me to take ownership of my pleasure. He didn't make it weird and he didn't ask to be involved in any way. It was something he did, just for me. And it worked – I experienced my first orgasm and didn't feel shame. The pleasure I felt was my human right and something my body had longed for.

I needed this shame to not show up when I considered having sex with people. And like all things I know little about, I did some research and asked friends who have more experience than I do. A friend sent me the book *Pleasure Activism: The Politics of Feeling Good* by Adrienne

Maree Brown, a book that encourages you to masturbate before you start reading and invites you to know yourself and be comfortable with desire and lust. Adrienne explores what it means to experience deep pleasure. She says that deep pleasure is felt when you ride the line between commitment and detachment; you commit yourself fully to the moment and you detach yourself from ego, shame and outcome. And that's what I needed to do: I needed to commit to my moments and the teachings I had of shame couldn't exist in those moments. What my mum, church or friends told me about sex shouldn't be in the moment. My fear of an unknown aftermath shouldn't be in the moment.

Contrary to what I had long believed, sex is for women and sex is for me. There's pleasure to be had in its spoken and unspoken beats: the lingering stares, the sound of heavy breathing, the seduction, the view of an aroused bulge, the anticipation. My body giving in and my head not getting in its way. I'm getting into erotica territory now but you get my point. I am excited for the sex that's to come, sex that feels good and where I am present and able to allow my body to feel all its pleasures.

✧

Audrey

I think we've all had that awkward experience of watching TV with our parents and a sex scene comes on the screen. I remember one occasion very clearly. I would've been about twelve at the time and the whole family was enjoying watching a Ghanaian film when the most awful sex scene came on. In true African style, the characters were over-exaggerating and doing the *most*. You couldn't see anything but the bed was shaking uncontrollably, and the characters were being loud. In the middle of the scene, I remember my mum randomly saying 'Oh wow he's really beating her up' to try and hide what was going on, but by this point, I was already watching the ten-minute free preview of the Fantasy Channel so I knew what was happening.

Sexuality in African culture is heavily rooted in patriarchy and follows specific biblical rules. Growing up in a Ghanaian household, sex wasn't something that was discussed openly. I don't think I heard the word *at all*. Add in the fact that I went to strict Catholic schools, primary and secondary, and this meant that it was always a very taboo subject. It wasn't always like this – before colonisation, Africans actually had a very liberal outlook on sexuality and, in some cultures, women were even allowed to have extra sexual lovers (including women). In my lifetime though, I was told that sex should come when you're married, not before. It's not until I was old enough to do the maths that I realised that I was at my parents' wedding, and similarly at the weddings of several aunties and uncles who loved to preach about purity, standing alongside with their own children. However, as an adult, I understand now it was a form of protection, trying to maintain our innocence.

I pretty much learned everything I knew about sex in teen magazines and problem pages. Problem pages were the part of the magazine where people would send their dilemmas in to an agony aunt for advice, very similar to what we do on *Your Receipts*. *More!* magazine was the most edgy teen mag and probably more suited to teenagers older than me, but I would buy it every week and skip straight to the sex position of the month and the problem pages. I'd read the magazine cover to cover then throw it in a bin outside so my mum didn't catch me.

> The 'birds and the bees' talk we see in the movies just wasn't something I experienced so I am grateful for the small guidance of magazines.

The 'birds and the bees' talk we see in the movies just wasn't something I experienced so I am grateful for the small guidance of magazines. My parents never sat me down to explain what sex was or the feelings that came attached to it. When you're the oldest out of your siblings, you have to find your own way through trial and error. I relied heavily on my friends and learned so much in the playground, even if I later grew up to find out most of it was fake news. For example, I was convinced that doggy style wasn't actually a sex position. The girls at primary school spoke with so much conviction that I really believed some of the things they revealed about boys, sex and relationships. I remember feeling so insignificant because I couldn't relate to what they were saying at all; my life still consisted of cartoons and hanging out with my siblings.

In Year 6, when one of the girls came on her period, I was genuinely confused because I had no clue what a period was at the tender age of ten. I remember being in the playground where one of the popular girls had everyone surrounding her as she explained she'd had her first period; she was now a woman and not a little girl like the rest of us. That evening, I went home and asked, 'Mummy, what's a period?' She asked me why I was asking and I explained about the girl at school. She replied, 'When you find blood in your knickers, come and find me and don't tell anyone else.' Three years later, that's exactly what happened. I still hadn't equated periods to sex or womanhood and my mum only elaborated by saying, 'You're a woman now' and that was the end of the discussion. This really was the extent of my sex education, growing up both at home and in school. I really wish I had someone to explain to me the emotional side of having sexual feelings, rather than just the physical act and the fact that you could get pregnant.

✧

I was a late bloomer when it came to boys and doing anything physical, but I always remember being extremely intrigued by sex and the way it made me feel. I never talked to anyone about it though because I thought I was perverted or weird. I had my first kiss at twelve and it was the most forced thing ever. A group of us used to walk home after school and go to this place called The Treehouse – it was literally a plank of wood in a tree – but we'd go there and hang after school. Most of my school life, I was the spectator never in the mix of anything, so during a game of truth or dare in The Treehouse when I had to kiss someone, it was a proper wet and messy snog. I had no clue what to do so I just replicated what I saw on TV. The next day I went to school and everyone was talking about it – I was mortified. I was never the person who got spoken about; I was usually doing the speaking. I'd never been so embarrassed in all my life but, like most gossip, it was forgotten about by the end of the day.

Growing up on a council estate, my parents really tried to shelter me from the outside world but, of course, as a kid, you are naturally curious. Most of my friends on the estate were sexually active from a young age and would tell me stories about their escapades. I would play it really cool but inside, I'd be dying of shock. By this point, I'd only gotten as far as kissing, so when they were divulging stories about sex in the park and blow jobs in the lifts, I couldn't believe it. My school experience and my life on the estate were completely juxtaposed; they were worlds apart. In a predominantly white school, I was invisible. At school, I had my crew, kept my head down and minded my business, but on the estate I had a bit more clout and sadly, this is where I developed my 'pick me' mentality. The boys I grew up with on my estate would purposely pit girls against each other and I used that to my advantage. When you're a horny teenager, all you care about is fitting in and getting attention from the opposite sex and I was no different. At the time, I wasn't aware that I was playing into the 'good girl' role, I just used what tools I had at my discretion. I'd get so gassed when I'd be described as 'wifey material', not knowing my value was being placed on my 'purity'.

The fact is, if I didn't have strict parents, I could've easily been sexually active from a young age, but having parents who kept constant tabs on me made it virtually impossible. I cringe so much now because at sixteen what the hell did I know about being a wife? I was a little girl subconsciously living through the male gaze. I think, from a very young age, men are aware of how to label women and put us in boxes and I utilised that at will. I'd do things like walk past the boys and accidently-on-purpose drop my school books to amplify my good girl image (I'm so embarrassed). One time, I was approached by a guy while I was walking through the estate when another man intervened and said, 'Nah, leave her alone, she's a good one' and I felt so good about myself. I consider myself now to be a reformed pick-me (a pick-me is a woman who does everything for the male gaze in the hopes of being chosen). I grew up and realised firstly, men ain't shit but secondly, all the performative behaviour I did for them never made me get chosen, so there was no reason for it. We live and we learn.

I lost my virginity a little later than most people, at the age of eighteen, and it was with a much older man. Looking back, I was probably 'groomed', but I didn't realise it at the time. He was someone I grew up with on the estate. He had moved away and lived on his own but would come back to see his mum most weekends. Like a typical lusty teenager, I had obsessed over him for years and he knew it. I'd accidently-on-purpose walk past his house when he was doing work on his car and he'd engage with me every time. Eventually, we exchanged numbers and he'd text me every time he was in the area. Then one day, I got the 'wanna link?' text and I lost my shit. I put on my Tammy Girl jeans and my FCUK t-shirt and went to meet him. He took me to his house and I lost my virginity to him. I think, deep down, I knew it would happen that day. I felt ready and it was with someone I really fancied. It didn't feel good at all; it just hurt and I bled so much. He dropped me home and I was convinced of two things: that my mum knew and that I was pregnant. Neither were true, thankfully.

✧

Audrey

My relationship with sex has evolved through experience. I remember having a friends-with-benefits situation and, from that experience, I realised I was able to detach sex from emotion if needs be. At first, I thought I was damaged because all I grew up hearing about was that sex and emotion go hand in hand, but I soon found out from talking to my friends that that isn't always the case. In fact, talking to my friends about sex has always been a kind of solace for me because, in being really open about it you come to learn that you're not alone in your thoughts at all.

Initially, I had a fear of talking about sex so much on the podcast because women get judged so harshly and are immediately labelled if they do so. But when you don't let labels define you, it can't offend you, especially when you've done the work to unlearn so many patriarchal tropes about sex. In turn, we've found that we've actually helped a lot of women to also be open about what they want and don't want in the bedroom. It's OK to masturbate, it's OK to not, it's OK to watch porn (within reason) and it's definitely OK to enjoy sex. I've talked about the 'hoe phase' so many times and this can often be misconstrued as advocating for promiscuity, but it really isn't. The hoe phase for one person might be dating and getting to know a number of

> When you don't let labels define you, it can't offend you, especially when you've done the work to unlearn so many patriarchal tropes about sex.

89

men or women simultaneously and, for another person, it might be casual sex with no strings attached as a way to get to know yourself and your body. As long as you're honest and safe, it's your body and your choice. However, what I would say is that before you embark on your hoe phase, you should know yourself and your boundaries. With sex, I think women can be shamed either way, because I've also seen modesty-shaming. Everything boils down to knowing yourself and it's definitely OK to feel that the sexual liberation movement isn't for you.

I feel like I've come full circle when it comes to my understanding of sex. On my journey of self-discovery, I realised that the ideologies that were passed on to me don't reflect how I feel about sex at all. Sexual liberation, for me, is having the agency to decide if you want to have sex or not. Sex isn't a gift we give to people as a reward. The power of sex comes in knowing that you have full agency over your body and that you get to choose who to give it to.

Milena

Sex? I don't even know what that is. I do not partake in such nastiness and, even if I did, one would never disclose such intimate moments! *Joking!* I'm more open than the pages of this book, *insert 'owwwweee' here*.

I honestly love and enjoy sex so much and I know the main reason for that is because I know and understand my body. I know what I like and how I like it, which makes sex all the more desirable. I think it's so important for women to get to know their bodies fully so they can enjoy sex as much as, if not more than, the person fucking them. I mean, shit, you want to

> I think the beauty of my generation and those coming after us is that we are actively starting to unravel all of these 'rules' around sex and sexuality.

be releasing that oxytocin too and not just with the shower head. I'm extremely sex positive and completely here for women normalising being vocal about wanting dick or vagina, as long as their partner is consenting and they are being safe. Who the fuck cares about what they do with their bodies? It is *theirs*!

For such a long time, women have been policed and looked down upon for having a sexual appetite. For the longest, we were made to believe that we were there to serve our partners (in many cultures, these views still, unfortunately, remain the same) and how dare we also want to be pleasured? I think the beauty of my generation and those coming after us is that we are actively starting to unravel all of these 'rules' around sex and sexuality. We're actually thinking about our own needs, wants and desires without feeling like a 'slag'. How about I can suck some dick and read a book too, it doesn't have to be either/or!

Coitus is absolutely amazing – I mean, not always, we've all probably had shit encounters that we'd rather forget about – but being intimate with somebody that you have a deep connection with is *out of this world*. I do think that sexual chemistry and a connection with somebody are two different things that I have definitely gotten confused in the past. I've been in positions (no pun intended) where the sexual chemistry is insane, but I don't want anything to do with that person beyond the bedroom door and that would always baffle me; I didn't understand how my juices could be flowing for someone and yet I couldn't see a future with them. I came to realise that my vagina and heart are like two different people (that bitch Heart needs to get a grip because Gina is just trying to have some fun). When you have that deeper level of understanding and commitment with somebody, chemistry comes naturally – you connect on many different levels and places deep within yourself are unlocked. Whereas, with chemistry on its own, you can feel drawn to someone physically but the emotional side can be very surface level. It doesn't take a lot to feel that magnetic pull of chemistry, and sometimes, emotional and physical wires can get crossed so I can see why it's difficult to differentiate the two.

Just like everyone else, I've been in awkward, funny, wild and beautiful sexual situations. However, one shit encounter always springs to mind. I was laying on my back and counting the squares on this guy's ceiling – it was 60 from what I can remember – and I genuinely have never felt boredom like that during sex *ever*. I would have rather redone my speed awareness course than have a repeat of that. What made it worse was that I knew he thought he was going in! My face had that 'what the fuck' look and I *refused* to fake-moan – I definitely wasn't wasting my vocals on such a shit shag especially when he didn't even touch the walls. I've never left a yard so quick in my life. It was so bad, I didn't even add him to my body count . . . such a waste of a sin.

Anyways, let me take you to more romantic times. I'll set the scene . . . I'm with a beautiful man in a stunning hotel for a weekend away. There's a bathtub big enough for the both of us in our room and it's filled with bubbles.

Sex

He pours me a glass of champagne and starts undressing. We get into the bathtub together and we are facing one another. Two hours pass and we're still in there, talking, laughing, drinking and listening to a playlist he put together for me. I remember the moment Snoh Aalegra's 'Find Someone Like You' came on and we just paused, looked deep in each other's eyes and took that moment to bask in it. It was perfect and the glimmer of the dimmed lights reflecting off of our naked wet bodies was doing bits! I felt like there was a whole zoo chilling in my stomach, not just some butterflies. I remember realising that it wasn't only sex, it felt different; the passion, love and emotions that oozed out of us were out of this world and we both felt it. I woke up in this stunning man's arms and he began to gently stroke my arm, then caressed my breasts and ran his fingertips down my body, gently pulled my undies aside before he slipped in. That first stroke was enough for me to never want to leave that bed – but we had to in the end because ain't *nobody* trying to lips with morning breath.

$$\diamond$$

My relationship with sex has not always been smooth sailing though, and for some, sex can be a very complicated and triggering thing. In the past, subconsciously, I started using sex as a form of control. If I was in a situation with a man where I knew he didn't want to be with me but I wanted him around, then I didn't care in what capacity I had him in my life just as long as I had him – sex was the only thing that would allow me to do that. It filled a void momentarily. It made me feel loved, I felt wanted and I yearned for that intimacy but afterwards, I would feel like absolute shit. It got too much for me to handle and I was forced to really look deep within myself and reflect on certain actions I was taking.

I've always had a very open relationship with sex (when I say that, I don't mean I'm out here moving reckless but even if I was, that's not your business). I talk about it very publicly and freely and I've never been afraid to express my wants and needs. I have been like this, even despite immature people who think that being sex positive automatically equates to being a 'hoe'.

However, one of the reasons I am so open might be because I was sexually abused as a child. It really shaped the relationship I have with sex, no matter how much I have tried to block it out. I think it made me feel that sex wasn't this sacred thing to me as my innocence had already been robbed, and so it made me explore things much earlier than I think I would have otherwise. This shit has been really hard to talk about and, in writing this, I've been forced to acknowledge it in black and white for the first time. It's brought up all of these emotions I had buried. One emotion that's imbedded into my core is anger. When you are a victim of abuse like this, you go through continual mental battles to process what you have experienced and you often sit there replaying what has happened over and over again.

My experience with men from the beginning was a mess, with no dad and suffering abuse, I learned men's capacity to leave, use and abuse woman very early on. However, instead of feeling like I was unable to trust men, I would run to them for that love and safety that I felt like I'd never had. I always felt like I was on a hunt for a protector, for somebody that would say to me, 'I've got you, you're safe now.' This explained why I always rushed into relationships and moved at a hundred miles per hour. Initially, I just thought it was me being a Libra (laughs in horoscopes), but I think I just used that as an excuse and a distraction from facing up to and acknowledging the core issue.

When I lost my virginity at fifteeen, at no point did I think of waiting until I was in a steady relationship, it was something I just wanted to get over and done with. In doing it I felt I had reclaimed my power and that I was back in control, it was my decision and I wanted it. Though in a way it was a good thing that I had gained a sense of ownership over my body, the reasoning behind it was because somebody else had had that authority over my body when I was younger, and they had taken my ability to choose away from me. It's only been recently that I've been able to be open about this. I've cried and cried until my eyes were raw because I had kept my mouth shut and repressed my past for so long. When I finally opened up, it felt like a weight had been lifted and that I could properly take action.

As a mother to a little girl, I wouldn't dare to think of what I'd do if she told me she experienced what I have in my life.

Milena

I certainly couldn't not believe her. I couldn't just brush it off because it happened many years ago. I couldn't negate her truth or not support how she wanted to handle things.

As I was writing this essay, I realised there was no way I could write about sex and not talk about the biggest thing that changed my life. I want to help other women who have stayed silent for so long and potentially empower them to speak out, as I know first-hand how damaging it is to suppress these experiences. I want to tell women that they aren't 'stained' or 'dirty' because of their abuse, and most importantly, I want to remind them that it wasn't their fault. I know what the right thing is for me to do now and I won't be silenced.

I am a survivor and I need to keep reminding myself of that.

✧

Mothering With Milena

Motherhood changed me completely and it's been a *journey*, one that nobody can prepare you for. However, there are a couple of things I wish I knew and I wish I had heard throughout my experiences as a mother so I've decided to be that voice for other mums and mums-to-be. Even if you only take one thing from this, I hope it makes you feel a little better and seen. I want to use this section to encourage, share some advice, normalise certain things and to help you understand that yes, you've had a child but, most importantly, *you are still a bad bitch.*

✧

Pregnant Mama

First of all, congratulations! You're growing a beautiful blessing inside of you. Every week, bebé gets bigger and bigger which may make things harder for you, but the beauty of it is that you're going to be able to feel them move, kick, hiccup and a lot more. At times – especially during the last four weeks – it is going to get tough, I know. You're going to feel exhausted, heavy and impatient but listen, you've grown a *full human being* inside of you, you are a wonder woman! Don't be hard on yourself, take deep breaths and meditate. Calm yourself where you can because any form of anxiety and stress can be passed on to baby.

The best advice I can give to a pregnant mama is to educate yourself, though, no matter how many *One Born Every Minute* episodes you watch, it won't prepare you for the thing, but it's still nice to see all the different ways labour can take you. As you reach different stages of your pregnancy, you will notice your body changing. Please do not feel disheartened if you see a few (or many) stretch marks on your bump, thighs, hips or butt. I think that sometimes we forget what our amazing bodies are actually doing. You are still beautiful and you should be so proud of yourself. We are all in different situations and I am aware that a pregnancy guide isn't one-size-fits-all so that's why you need to do what *makes you* happy and focus on what makes *you* comfortable. It's not easy, but you got this.

Mama To A Newborn

First off, YOU FUCKING DID IT – well done sweetie! Whether it was vaginal or a C-section, you still did that. If your birthing plan went out of the window, that's OK and it doesn't mean that you have failed. Regardless, the most important thing is that your baby is here. I know a lot of women go into labour with a plan, with every detail organised and a clear vision of how they want their gorgeous baby to come into the world, but the reality is that your body and your child are going to do whatever they need to in order to get into the world quickly and safely. Try to accept your labour (or seek therapy if it was difficult) and focus on your newborn.

Please do not feel pressure to breastfeed or to have a house full of visitors. Let people know your boundaries. Even if they don't understand it, stand firm because they weren't the one who just gave birth so they need to chill out. Your sleep is going to be broken and you'll probably be feeling the after-effects of the birth – whether that's still feeling random contractions, bleeding, healing stitches either down below or your C-section. Just take your time. Even if you are not experiencing any of these things, you're still definitely not going to be 'back to normal' in a day or even a few months, so be kind to yourself. Never feel afraid to ask for help or to take a break.

Mama Guilt

When I first had Cataleya, the body and mind that I was left with felt foreign to me. I loved her so much, but I knew that mentally I wasn't 100% happy. That took a lot to admit because I felt so guilty. I'd say to myself, 'There are women who aren't able to have kids, fix up!' I wasn't understanding that what I was feeling was valid and I didn't need to compare. Sadly, I didn't enjoy my pregnancy for the most part and, at times, I felt trapped. I knew that, in order for me to give my baby the best version of me, I needed a break to get my shit together.

I went away when she was three-months old because I was suffering from post-natal depression. A lot of other mums and people judged me on my decision, but I just knew that I was doing the right thing for me and my family. I will always be grateful to my mum for supporting me and looking after Cataleya during that time. When I got back, I realised that if I hadn't taken that moment for me, I probably would have had a complete breakdown. From then on, I knew that, though everybody was going to have an opinion on my parenting, it meant nothing as long as my child was happy and healthy. Never feel guilty for not taking the same routes as other mums. Though this is just one example of this guilt, I've experienced it many more times since then. I imagine I'll always have that little voice in my head making me second-guess myself but we all need to remember that you cannot please everybody and to trust our instincts.

Mama Gone Wild

How dare mums go out raving? They should be at home in their onesies, drinking tea and being a mum! *Wrong*. Becoming a mum doesn't mean leaving the fun behind. I've never seen having kids as a jail sentence. I truly believe that you can still do you and be a parent, you just have to be mindful. You have to realise that you have this new responsibility that ranks incredibly high on your priority list, but that doesn't mean throwing your social life in the bin. Wanting to go to the club and have a drink doesn't have to stop if you don't want it to. If you do want it to stop, then that's also your prerogative and also OK. I hate the fact that a lot of mums feel like they can't be 'too wild' or 'too sexy' because that would somehow detract from their mothering skills, when, in fact, it is healthy to go out and feel liberated for a few hours when you want it.

This also applies to sex. When it comes to all mums talking about sex or having sex, it's still such a taboo. Not a lot of women like to discuss it as they don't want to be deemed as a 'bad example to their kids' or 'a slut'. I'm sorry but my sexual desires didn't pack up and leave the moment I conceived and, therefore, if I choose to have sex and talk about it, I am entitled to. Getting my ass tapped doesn't make me a bad mother. On another hand, there are a lot of women that feel like they have lost their mojo; they're not comfortable in their bodies and sex is the last thing on their minds. A way to get through this is by taking the time to pleasure yourself, it's definitely worth the energy!

Mama Still Loves Herself

We focus so hard on being a mum, a partner, a nurturer, and a carer, that we forget that, before being a mother, we were us. We put all of our wants and needs on a back burner and give our all to raising this child but we forget that, in order for our baby to be happy, we have to be happy too.

Loving myself is a journey that I feel like I'll be on forever but every day, I actively work to feel more comfortable with me. I've come a long way from where I first started out. I know that the more I read affirmations out loud to myself and actually take the time that I need to understand myself, the more I'll continue to feel and be better, but it's a process. Do whatever it is that you need to do to be happy and do not feel bad for wanting to be selfish. We all have different things that make us happy and they don't have to be extravagant – I know the first time I did a shit in peace, I felt like I had won the lottery! Try writing down all the things that make you happy – it could be having a bath, ordering your favourite take out or pampering yourself – and tick it off like a bucket list, except it's a regular thing you do.

After having Cataleya, I always wondered if I'd ever feel as I did before being a mum and it was a thought that would often get me down. I'd constantly reminisce on the days where I was young and free, not realising that I was still able to feel that sense of freedom as a mum. Slowly and surely, I realised that putting me first doesn't mean that I am putting motherhood last.

Mama Trying to Maintain Her Relationship or Find Love

When you're a new parent, you tend to neglect your partner. We are all guilty of it. We're too wrapped up in our bundle of joy that we forget what else is important. A piece of advice that I'd give to couples with a newborn is to not forget about each other. Spend time together and that doesn't just mean being in the same room – we all know you can be surrounded by people and still feel lonely. Make sure you interact and absorb the moments you both have created. Date nights are also so important. You both should still be making an effort for one another and yes, I know you're tired and you can't be bothered, but the simple things can go a *long* way.

Now, if you're single with a child or children, please do not feel like you are tainted goods. I felt like this for the longest and thought the easiest thing to do would be to just stay with my baby father, even though I was unhappy. I kept thinking, 'Who would want a woman with a baby?' But do you know who I realised would want me? *The right person for me.* Do not rush into things. Really acknowledge your amazing qualities so that you don't feel deflated. I'll admit, dabbling in the jungle while having a child is a challenge, but it will all come together eventually. I think having an understanding with your child's other parent is key, though if they're not somebody that wants to cooperate, please do not let this stop you from pursuing love.

Unfortunately, there will be people that may decide that you're not for them when they learn you have a child – so you just have to punch them in the face. *Joking*. I just wanted to make you smile if you felt triggered. Please don't let this dishearten you. Everybody has a different outlook or way they envisage their future, so just see it as a piece of puzzle that doesn't fit your board and keep it moving, mamacita!

Mama and Her Dreams

Working on your career and pursuing your dreams feels like a long shot when you've become a mum. You start wondering where you'll find the time, especially as you don't want to leave your baby because you don't want to miss a single thing. I want everybody reading this to know that you can shape your child's future without being right next to them all the time. It's all about allowing yourself the time to better yourself. In doing that, not only do you gain knowledge and experience, you will also learn incredible things that you can then pass on to you kids when they get older.

I remember going on *The Receipts Podcast* tour, our first ever UK tour, and I didn't know how I was going to cope with being away every weekend for two months, as well as a couple of days during the week where I was recording the podcast and doing interviews. I can't lie, it was hard. Thank God I had her dad and my family to help. I felt like every time I got home, I was leaving again but I always explained to her where I was going and the reasons why. I wanted her to know that I was working for her and us. It's important that you explain these things to your kids so they don't feel like you've just 'abandoned' them. You are working hard for a reason: for a better future for your family. That is worth it.

✧

Tolly

My therapist once told me to stand in my capital 'I' and I nodded along, pretending I understood what she was talking about. She said that I had a habit of standing in my small 'i', to which I responded with a blank face. She carried on talking and explained that I knew who I was and what I wanted, but I was too scared to stand in it fully. My version of myself was created through everyone else's lenses and I didn't know what the vision looked like through just mine.

I allowed other people's labels to tell me who I am and those labels varied. They ranged from 'mean girl' to 'strong woman' to 'cocky'. I would take on these labels and wear them – even though they didn't fit me, even when they felt too tight, too restrictive. I would wear them because it meant I didn't have to label my true self; it meant that she could be left inside me, without me having to do the work to find her. Finding yourself is a pretty big task, one that I am not sure is actually possible, because we are constantly evolving. Who I am now is not who I was in my twenties, and I am sure I will read this book back one day and realise that I have changed again. I have evolved, I have had conversations that rocked my world and felt feelings that have changed my mind. Maybe allowing myself to change and evolve is part of the journey to finding me.

✧

I have always found the idea of people going away to find themselves amusing. It felt self-indulgent and I didn't understand why self-discovery had to happen in Thailand. But, as self-centred as finding yourself seems, it is necessary. It is important to be selfish with this goal because, at the root of everything you do, is who you are. Knowing who I am, what I value and what I have to offer makes my world make sense. It's made me a better friend, sister, daughter and person. But this journey is hard, and it involves breaking down. Breakdown for me didn't include the familiar tropes: I didn't cut my hair and I didn't have that moment where I laid in bed, bottle of alcohol in hand and smudged make-up on my face. It didn't even happen after a life-changing event where no one but me knew I was going through it.

I feel like my breakdown creeped up on me. It happened at what looked like the best time of my life. I was successful, I was having a good time, and yet, I had this feeling that something wasn't right. The more I ignored it, the bigger it got, until it got so big, it overwhelmed me. It was like my body, my energy and my inner self were all telling me that we couldn't carry on like this. Me to me was like 'Sis, we are not OK, look after us. Stop trying to push this down. *Prioritise us.'*

During my breakdown, I kept saying to myself that I just needed a hug, a hug that could reach so deep, it would feel like it was holding me together. I don't like to admit that I need people because it makes me feel weak and neediness has never been a trait I could dabble in. I never had the privilege to be needy. Mum was working to provide for us and we had to be self-sufficient. But, in this moment, I needed help. I needed to be nurtured.

> I kept saying to myself that I just needed a hug, a hug that could reach so deep, it would feel like it was holding me together.

The breakdown meant that I had to shed layers; I was dropping things that no longer served me. I realised that the ways I had always dealt with things were no longer working, and when I say 'I realised', I mean my therapist made it clear to me. I couldn't plaster everything with 'we move' because, often, I had to stop, reflect and feel.

After the breakdown comes the building up, another over-whelming yet rewarding task. You have to start figuring out what feels good, what you're passionate about, what works for you and how to live a life that is centred around you. And you're attempting all of this in a world where you have consistently been told that being selfish is wrong. My world has always made me feel like I have the obligation to bring my community along with me, so being self-centred and standing in my capital 'I' is difficult for me. I had to learn, and I am still learning, how to explore myself with the same fascination I have for new friends. I have had to become curious about myself, to know what I want, to know what feels good and what doesn't. The more my fascination with myself grew, the more questions I had to ask myself, and I would ask these questions out loud:

* What do you want?

* What do you love?

* What are you good at?

* What does the world need?

* Who are you?

* Who are the people you feel the happiest around?

* What was the last thing that made you excited?

* What's one thing you're sure about?

The building up also included learning to forgive myself for past mistakes. Mistakes that felt like I didn't look out for my own best interests. Mistakes like dating and trusting the wrong people. I would think about these mistakes and have an overwhelming sense of shame. Shame serves very little purpose. It makes you want to hide away and not deal with the situation. Shame often doesn't leave a gap for healing. I learned that being disappointed in myself doesn't have to look like shame. Also, these errors and mistakes I have made don't define me. Instead of sitting in the mistakes and being embarrassed by them, I had to learn from them. Loving myself looks like forgiving myself; to learn to like me, flaws and all.

✧

When I think about loving myself, William Bell's 'I Forgot to Be Your Lover' comes to mind. William Bell wasn't talking about self-love in his song and, rather, he was singing about how he neglected his partner. He starts the song by asking her if he had told her lately that he loved her. And then, he spends the rest of the song berating himself for letting life get in the way of him being her lover. He talks about how he didn't put his arms around her when she needed it and promised to spend the rest of his life making it up to her. Jaheim later sampled the song and called his version 'Put That Woman First'.

This song makes me realise that I sometimes forget to be my own lover and that I let life get in the way. I let attaining goals, work and trauma get in the way of loving me. And, just like William Bell, I have now promised to spend the rest of my life making up for that. I have to over-compensate for the times I concentrated on the parts of me that I didn't like. Make up for all the negative things I have told myself, about myself. I had to start looking after myself and love me like my life depends on it, because ultimately it does. I also had to start believing that I was deserving of what I have and what I desire. *The Receipts*

Podcast should be successful because we have worked hard for it. I am deserving of the amazing opportunities I have been given and I should be in the rooms I am in. I am beautiful and worthy of the man I envisage myself with.

✧

My therapist has been critical in the journey to finding myself and from our earliest session, she made it clear to me that this is something we had to do. She once ended a session by saying 'look after yourself' and I replied, 'What does that look like?' We are often told to look after ourselves and, to me, it always sounded like a passing comment, just another way to end a conversation. A well wish, I guess. She replied that looking after myself involved me being in tune with myself and she encouraged me to check in with myself. And you know what? Sis is worth every penny. The simple act of just asking myself 'How are you?' has allowed me to know what I need. And often, what I need is kindness. A lot of my self-care includes compassion for myself. Self-care and self-love are in the little things I do for myself: making sure I am getting a good night's sleep, eating on time, resting guilt-free, dressing well and moving – the latter looks like dancing around my house and using the mirror to see what it looks like when I'm throwing it back.

> The simple act of just asking myself 'How are you?' has allowed me to know what I need.

Self-love, self-acceptance and self-confidence are not things that society wishes for you, unless they come with a product they can sell. They are especially not things they want for Black women. I have always used my voice – to ask questions and to cause trouble – and I've also always had a sense of confidence; a confidence that has made people feel uncomfortable. People are uncomfortable with a confidence they didn't help you build. They don't understand why you believe in your own sauce and why you don't need validation from them. As a result, they try to knock it out of you, while trying to project their insecurities onto you. But I'm going to pass on that and continue to pass on it. If you know how long it took me to love me, you will understand why my confidence is independent of the opinions of others. I can't act like I don't care what anyone thinks because that would be a lie. I care about the opinions of the people that love me and I care about what people think of my work, but what is completely irrelevant is anyone who is trying to make me doubt who the fuck I am.

I have always wanted to be like the confident Black women I saw growing up; these women were so magnetic to me and these women were within reach of me. I saw confidence in my mum, in my aunties, and that basketball coach that trained me once. I remember when she walked into the sports hall that day and she was beautiful. She had her hair out in an afro and she commanded the attention of the room with her confidence alone. When she spoke, with her voice filling up the whole hall, she had that ability to make you feel like she was talking just to you. I was so in awe of her, I wondered if I fancied her. But I have since had this feeling for many women and it's a feeling of adoration that comes from rating and respecting them. Seeing these women and watching how they move through life has allowed me to form the type of life I want for myself. I want a full life, one that I am proud of and one that feels good. I want to know that I loved and felt love. I want to fulfil my dreams, I am dedicated to fulfilling these dreams.

Through the process of learning to stand in my capital 'I', I have learned to be confident in my light and magic. I seldom talk like this, because it feels indulgent and a little airy-fairy, but I know I have something special within me. I call it 'the God in me' and, even when I don't see it, people point it out to me. I know deep down that God didn't put me on this earth to be ordinary, nor did he put me here to hide away in the corner. My light is not a dull flicker, it's so bright it allows people to bask in it; it allows them to feel seen in it. And even in times when the world seems dark, this inner light has brought me hope and comfort and I vow to nourish it so I can watch it get brighter and stronger.

✧

Audrey

As with most people, my childhood played a huge role in who I have become. I've always considered myself to be very privileged in terms of how I grew up. When I talk about privilege, I don't mean money because I definitely did not grow up rich – far from it, in fact. I didn't realise that we were working class, or maybe even poor, until I got much older. My parents both worked hard in their respective fields and it's only now, as an adult, that I'm able to see how they elevated themselves from where they started out.

When my mum first came to the UK in 1984, she worked in Wimpy and my dad in John Lewis, but they both studied and later on my mum qualified as a midwife and my dad as a social worker. They worked their asses off to get us off the council estate I grew up on. My little brother was getting older and they were determined to make sure he wouldn't fall in with the wrong crowd and, as small as it sounds, they always wanted a house with a garden. Of course, it wasn't perfect, however, my parents really did everything in their power to make life comfortable for my siblings and me throughout our childhoods. Most of my friends and family come from single-parent households, or their parents split up when they were young, or they didn't grow up with their dad in the house – in a sense, I was a bit of a unicorn, especially because my dad was also very present in the home. I believe all these elements have shaped the woman that I am today, including my positive attitude, balanced and incredibly tolerant qualities, which boil down to this upbringing.

✧

Young Audrey was multifaceted, even as a little girl. I exuded so much confidence and energy and I remember really enjoying my own company.

Though I was confident for the most part, I recently saw pictures of myself aged six with a towel on my head trying to look like I had long flowing hair like my white peers. When I see pictures like that, it makes me sad. As innocent as it was, I see how problematic it really is and it's crazy how, even as a young child, you can discern what 'pretty' is and find creative ways to emulate it. I know, as a young girl, I was so conflicted: I remember often hearing whispers from family members about how much of a cute kid I was, then going to school and not feeling that way at all. At that age, I couldn't articulate that it was my Blackness that made me 'unpretty' amongst my school mates – I just knew that I wasn't the same.

Audrey

As I got older, I realised that it wasn't going to be my looks that got me far in life. The environment I grew up in was what, ultimately, taught me this. Being one of the only Black people in spaces for most of my life, and because my understanding of racism was very surface-level, I chose to handle my difference by being 'the good Black'. I internalised this so much, I believe it made me into a people pleaser, and even occasionally a bit of a pushover, because I really didn't want to become a stereotype. In a way, I think this has stopped me accessing my full humanity: what would I be like if I didn't have to live my life this way? Is it nature or nurture that made me feel like this? I've talked many times about suffering from imposter syndrome, and I remember how happy I was when, in my late twenties, I found out there was a name for how I'd felt for so many years.

I also began to give more thought to the qualities I possess – the good, the bad and the ugly – in my late twenties and to take practical steps towards changing the things I didn't like about myself. I think it's important to stop and give yourself an evaluation to help with self-evolution. It can be so easy to get lost in this world, especially with how fast-paced life can be. We can get so caught up in our lives that we don't stop to take things in and actually reflect, especially considering how much we consume through social media. I realised recently that, because of social media, I couldn't remember what it felt like to be bored; we have so many distractions available to us, all you have to do is pick up your phone and you can be provided with instant entertainment.

If 2020 taught me anything, it was the importance of stopping and taking time to self-analyse. I didn't realise how many things I had put on the back burner and hadn't nurtured because I was so busy all of the time – one of the most significant of those things was my mental health. I'd previously never paid attention to my mental health much because I considered myself to be someone who was lucky enough to have solid mental health. A coping mechanism for me has always been the idea that someone else has it worse so I don't have anything to complain about. I've always been able to compartmentalise my emotions and deal with things as and when I feel ready – I don't know if that's a blessing or a curse. I'm the type of person who can be feeling sad and depressed and the world would never know. I've never liked the idea of taking my moods out on other people so I'd rather hone in on something that makes me happy in the moment and deal with my issues later, or fake it till I make it. I later realised that I wasn't dealing with anything, instead I was suppressing it.

Going from being super busy to being confined to my house was hard and I was forced to deal with a lot of things I'd pushed to the back of my head.

When everything stopped during lockdown and there was nowhere to go and nothing to do but think, it made me go a little crazy. Lockdown really took its toll on me. Going from being super busy to being confined to my house was hard and I was forced to deal with a lot of things I'd pushed to the back of my head. I realised why it had been so necessary that I was always busy – I find resting difficult. It's rare that I'll have a lie-in or just spend the day on the couch. I feel like there's always something that needs doing and even if there isn't, I'll create work for myself. I wanted to understand why I always felt the need to be distracted; what exactly was it that I was running away from? I decided to look into it further and speak to a therapist.

Having a unbiased stranger to vent to felt amazing. I would just talk, and my therapist would just listen with no judgements or interruptions and that was exactly what I needed. I wanted to take the measures and jump in front of a problem before it arose. Essentially, I used therapy as a preventative measure, which is perfectly fine to do. One of the things I wanted help with was how to deal with becoming increasingly visible as *The Receipts Podcast* became more and more popular. As the podcast grows, so does the pressure of what people want from you and, as a people pleaser, this can be quite dangerous.

When the podcast first launched, we all agreed that we'd be as transparent as possible and give our audience our authentic selves, but it was very easy to agree this when there were no expectations. I talk quite freely and giving so much of myself felt natural and therapeutic. Luckily, so far, the listeners seem to love it and, four years in, we've been so blessed to receive such a warm reception. That being said, I've always been conscious that this could change with one tweet, comment or opinion, especially in an age of 'cancel culture'. It's long been a fear of mine and this was something I wanted to unpack in therapy. Even though four years is a long time and we've worked hard and given so much, it's still scary to think it can all be snatched away from you at any minute. I've seen it happen to other people – some bounce back and others don't. I've always felt so grateful to be given such an amazing opportunity and I really don't want to fumble it in any way – especially not in a self-inflicted fumble.

When I eventually did speak to my therapist about this she wanted to get the bottom of where the fear stemmed from. She encouraged me to make a plan and be secure in it. She also wanted me to understand that not everything is meant to last forever and that's OK. What we've achieved will leave behind a legacy, even when we're no longer as visible, and that made me feel really good and at peace with my fear. I've learned so much about myself through this process, and in case they can help you, some of the biggest teachings for me have been:

* Be easier on yourself. It's OK to not be OK. Don't be hard on yourself if you don't complete everything on your to do list, or if you miss an appointment or if you don't achieve your goals for the week.

* Learn to say no without guilt. Putting yourself first is a positive thing and sometimes you can't make yourself available to everyone who might need you.

Audrey

* Don't hold things in too much because a problem shared is a problem halved. Speak to people you trust because letting it out can sometimes help.

* Don't sweep things under the carpet, tackle them head on when the time feels right. You don't have to resolve everything straight away, but make sure you do if it becomes too much to carry.

✧

On the podcast, we get asked so much about confidence and self-love because, unintentionally, these are the biggest messages to come from *The Receipts*. When we realised that's what young women were taking from it, it made my heart burst with joy because loving yourself just isn't something we're taught. People ask me how and why I'm so confident and I always say that it's something that's come with age; the older I've gotten, the more I've learned to accept myself in all my glory. I developed a 'like me or leave me' attitude and it stuck. Growing up without social media meant that I wasn't under the same pressures that young women face today. Thankfully, there was no Instagram, so I wasn't bombarded with images of perfect-looking people every day. However, even at my big age of thirty-five, it still affects me so I can only imagine what it feels like for young girls.

I like to give actual practical things you can do to tap into self-confidence because it's really easy to just say love yourself but how do you actually accomplish this? Here are some tips:

* Make sure you control what you're consuming on socials – the algorithm only shows us what we want to see so unfollow, mute and hide anything that doesn't serve you. Follow accounts that uplift and represent you.

* Remember that people are only showing their wins and highlights on socials and that it's all an illusion.

* Confidence isn't built overnight so don't beat yourself up because you're not there yet, I promise you, it's a journey.

* The key to loving yourself is to take each day as it comes, but you can start by finding one thing you love about yourself and accentuating that.

* In an era where having an hourglass insta body is all the rage, it's hard not to get caught up in image and how you look. I *do not* have this body type, but I highlight my strong points (great legs and boobs hahaha) and for you, it might be your eyes and hair. Whatever the combo is, do something to highlight that part of you and I promise you'll exude a different kind of energy.

* It's not all about how you look. Focusing on bettering yourself by learning more or laughing more is just as good as putting on eyelashes.

Audrey

* Hone in on the part of your personality that makes you stand out and makes you unique. Try to amplify that – what does interesting look like to you? Don't try to be anyone else as they're already taken.

✧

I've always said that I want to be chosen because then you know the person actually wants to be there, but as I'm getting older, I'm realising that you have to also take control and ultimately choose yourself. I've never ever been a risk taker, and rather, I'm someone who very much does things by the book, but 2020 taught me that life is too short. You have to go for the things you want in life and getting knocked back doesn't make you a failure.

When I think about Audrey today, I'm proud of her. She's surprised me in ways I didn't think were possible.

✧

Milena

We spend most of our lives helping and advising others and forget to do the same for ourselves. We spend all day every day with our minds and yet, we don't take the time to make them a beautiful and comfortable place to be. This is why some of us are so scared of spending time on our own or to look at our own reflection. It takes a lot to look within and start unpacking certain truths in order to move forward and break cycles. I feel like growing up, I always felt a little lost. I knew I wasn't 100% inside but I always just got on with it.

> We spend all day every day with our minds and yet, we don't take the time to make them a beautiful and comfortable place to be.

During the first lockdown of 2020, my mental health deteriorated. I had been suffering with health anxiety for three years by that point and, though I had done CBT (Cognitive Behavioural Therapy) and other forms of therapy, I still felt like there was a lot more I had to deal with in order to blossom as a person.

I knew I needed to take ten steps back in order to move forward and that it would be a hard process, but I saw therapy in the same way as when you need to sort your room: it gets messier before it's all clean and organised. I felt so ready to learn about me, and I'm so glad I did.

If I could go back a few years and talk to myself when I was going through it, this is what I would say:

Milena, it's OK.

I promise you: you will be OK. This is all temporary but you have to go through the motions, ride the wave like you been riding the dick and learn from it all. First things first, you can't bury your feelings any more. You've done such a great job of masking it all that you deserve an award! However, you need to acknowledge your childhood in order to move forward and no, this doesn't make you a 'victim' nor is it an excuse for certain behaviours. That being said, your childhood experiences have shaped you. You need to acknowledge them so you can figure out what you want to keep, what you need to work on and what you have to get rid of. It'll be a bit like when you're going through your wardrobe and having a clear out.

I know you've always felt the need to prove yourself and that you're not good enough, but without you knowing, this has stemmed from feelings you had at a very early age. It was easier for you to blame yourself for not having your parents with you rather than painting them in a negative light. You placed your self-worth on their actions, and it made you feel like you weren't worthy. You were a four year old that just needed to be held and loved. You had your Aunty Mia and Uncle Niall who absolutely adored you, well, when you weren't 'howling' as Uncle Niall would say. With their love, they were trying to overcompensate for the lack of stability that you had, and in the end, they made you quite spoilt! Looking back, you were a crybaby – you were crying because you were so afraid of being abandoned. Let's not forget, you went to four different primary schools in a short space of time. You were constantly meeting new kids and trying to make friends and, even though you felt scared, there wasn't any time to feel that. You had a small window to make a good impression so you had to appear confident. Showing everybody you could sing was your go-to and it worked, every single time, but doing that instead of feeling the feels wasn't healthy. You were always forced to adjust and that has been true across your whole life. You've been a chameleon. Boy George up in this bitch.

I need you to know that you are wanted, you're needed and that you're enough – for Cataleya, for your family, for your friends and for the podcast. Stop second-guessing yourself and thinking that if you walked away, people wouldn't notice. You bring so much to people's lives without even knowing it. Looking back, you always wanted to be the centre of attention and, to a certain extent, you still do now. Back then, it was because you didn't want to feel forgotten about when, in reality, being recognised doesn't always mean being the main act. It was a cry for help, a cry for amor. Therapy has really changed you; you're going to have many realisations and epiphanies, things will suddenly make complete sense to you. You're going to start to become the woman you've always been destined to be. You're going to begin to love yourself more instead of putting your energy into short-fused loves that only leave you broken. You'll learn that they just leave you with that same empty hole.

Talking about voids, you've finally gotten rid of a man that never chose you but sold you all the dreams. You weren't rich so I never really understood how and why you kept buying that crap; coming like loo roll in 2020, you'd bulk buy his bullshit! How could you not? He told you everything you wanted to hear and it meant nothing whether it was the truth or not because his girl was right there next to him, not you. It won't be until you have a session with your therapist, and she asks you, 'What is it about him you want?' And your answer is 'I want him to see that I could be the one' that you will see the reality of the situation. I know you could never understand why he wouldn't leave the entanglement he was in when he 'loved you' and 'couldn't imagine his life without you in it', but the truth is that you wanted that relationship to work out so badly, you ignored the negative things and made excuses. The only reason you kept forgiving him for his fuckboy antics was because he, at least, used to apologise and acknowledge how you felt – more than you had been used to in the past.

Let me tell you your friends are beyond fucking ecstatic that you've finally moved on. They didn't know how much more they could take (and that's without the extra shit you didn't tell them about). They were so over giving you all the advice and you going ahead and doing whatever it is you wanted to do! After that therapy session, you will feel overwhelmed with all of the pieces of the puzzle coming together because moving on is hard. You will want to punch up your therapist but also hug her all at once. You will go to the studio that evening and cry, but you know what? We thank God because that evening, you'll create magic and one of your dearest songs to your heart, 'Daddy Issues'. You're so lucky that you always have music to escape the madness of the world.

With your music, you will finally go back in the studio and be able to focus on your first love. You've been singing since the moment you could talk. You've always known that you wanted to be a singer but you lost all of your confidence after having Cataleya. I know anxiety has weighed on you like a ton of bricks but it's good that you're pushing yourself. People are waiting for you and there is no way you can let that voice go to waste (that mouth been doing bits though, oweee!).

Your confidence will go up again. You first got into podcasting because you were looking for somewhere to help you regain it. It was therapeutic for you, sitting in front of a mic with three girls you had only just met and sharing your experiences. I know now that you feel anxious about being on there and I've noticed there are times where you haven't been completely yourself. You hold back and, instead of opening your mouth, you'd rather stay silent. You know why that *is – you're afraid. You overthink everything, from simple things like interviews and introducing guests to improvising for a video. If it's not perfect, you panic and shut down. In your mind, make one wrong move and that's it, it could be a mess. So instead of trying and fucking up, you'd rather keep your mouth closed, just in case you come across as 'dumb' or you 'don't get it right'. You don't want people to think badly of you but you're starting to learn that people will have their opinions regardless.*

You've become a brand and it's been difficult to manage that, as you know every little thing could potentially be scrutinised and these fears go back to your childhood of always wanting to be accepted. The truth is, you're not everybody's cup of tea and that's cool, who gives a fuck? You cannot live your life dulling yourself down because you want to please everybody. Imagine them all being content with you yet you're completely sad within? That's all-mad mate, be you! There are so many that relate to you and so many women you represent and speak for. I'm glad that you're finally focusing on what YOU think and feel and you've recognised that you're very much needed.

Love, Milena.

✧

Working on yourself is one of the hardest challenges ever yet can also be so rewarding. Accepting your flaws and having to really face the music isn't easy but it has to be done if you want to flourish in this life. There are cycles that need to be broken and it wasn't until I saw a quote that said 'we end up in therapy because our parents didn't go' that I thought I have a real duty here, not just to myself, but to my kids. Going to therapy means that I'll have better techniques to handle certain things in my future and the ability to really sit down and think before reacting. Self-reflection is key, and I hope mine will inspire you to do the same.

Therapy has really changed my life and the way I rant and rave about it, you'd think I'd have fucking shares in the industry. I just think it's so important to do, especially if you want to be a better human being. A lot of people think that, because they're not on their last leg or because their lives are great, they don't need it but I've learned that your vida doesn't have to be a shitshow in order to need somebody to talk to. Your life doesn't have to be crumbling before your eyes to make you want to vent to somebody in a safe zone. If I didn't do it, I would still be constantly hurting myself and then teaching my daughter the same shit. I knew I had to get it together for her, because I wouldn't forgive myself if she grew up and had the same issues as me. I've decided I'm going to be that comfortable outlet for her. I wasn't granted that openness from my family so I'm

> Your life doesn't have to be crumbling before your eyes to make you want to vent to somebody in a safe zone.

going to make sure that my daughter knows that she can come to me for anything and that I'll be strong enough to be able to guide her. She's got a pretty lit mama after all.

✧

Affirmations

There's plenty more dick in the sea.

There has to be a time where you realise that there's more men out there than the one who let you down. That person may not have been for you, but there is somebody out there who is.

Life is for the living.

This is both a fact and an affirmation that encourages you to live life and to live it to its fullest and its truest. Everything you do in life kneels to the intention that 'life is for the living' and you are going to live the very best version of it.

If you live by a person's compliments, you'll die by their criticism.

Do not place your value on other's opinions of you. Be confident and secure in yourself to the point where if anybody leaves your life you are still able to stand on your own two feet.

What is for you will not pass you by, nurture your own blessings and spend less time watching other peoples'.

Sometimes we become so obsessed with watching other peoples' lives we forget to live our own and don't realise the blessings we have in front of us. When you feel yourself doing this make sure you check yourself.

An ant can do more on its feet than an elephant lying down.

An old Ghanian proverb that means little by little, if you are determined and diligent, you can accomplish great things. Small wins can add up to a big success.

Pay attention to people's actions and not their words.

People can say whatever they want to you without actually doing jack shit. Take everything said with a pinch of salt and watch what people show you and their intentions will become very clear.

I will not contort, minimise or dim who I am or what I want for the benefit of anyone.

There's something powerful about choosing to be audaciously you. It says that you will not shrink who you are, nor will you mould or bend to fit into the box society has made for you. It is a form of freedom; it says that you are not ashamed of your heart's desires.

Thou shall not put men before life experiences.

Try not to choose time with a man over experiences or let a man's opinion hold you back. Memories last forever and men don't in most cases.

Don't let age be a roadblock to following your dreams.

It's easy to let your age hold you back. There'll always be people who tell you you're too old to do something or that you should be at a certain place in your life because of your age and it is bullshit. Experience everything you want, whenever you want, the world is your oyster.

I can't come and die.

You are worthy of rest. Good things don't come hand in hand with stress and struggle. It's OK to let go of things that are more effort than they're worth.

Self-love is a marathon, not a sprint – it won't happen overnight.

Self-love is a constant journey, you never get to a final destination, and so it's OK to have shit days. Just try not to let the bad overtake the good.

Tolly

I remember telling Anita, my college media teacher, that I wanted to be a WAG when I grew up. It was 2006, I was sixteen, and the wives and girlfriends of high-profile footballers, or WAGs as they were referred to, reigned supreme. It's worth noting that the World Cup had just happened, England had gotten to the quarterfinals, and the WAGs were on the cover of every magazine, with Victoria Beckham, Coleen Rooney and Cheryl Cole being the most elite. Even though I was partly joking when I said it, I really wouldn't have minded being dressed in a miniskirt, designer sunglasses and real UGG® boots, cheering on my footballer husband. Anita asked me to stay behind after class that day – she wanted to talk me out of this WAG dream. Although sweet, her concern wasn't necessary. The idolisation of WAGs quickly died out and it was no longer cool to be labelled according to your association to a man. So I had to revert back to my actual dream job, which didn't include me spending my days shopping, or at a salon getting my nails done. I was going to be a writer and have my own magazine one day – that was the real dream.

But, of course, no kid says 'writer' when asked what they want to be when they grow up. So, like all kids, I went through a whole list of possible career options. I wanted to be a pilot, but that quickly fizzled out and was probably linked to my longing to be close to my dad who was a pilot. Once the pilot dream died, I wanted to be a fashion designer and I am sure I was the first to design skousers, you know, the combination of a skirt and trousers that was a nineties wardrobe staple. With no actual real plan on how to make this happen, this dream also died. Then I started writing scripts, although I don't think I knew they were scripts at the time. I would go home and write about what happened in my day, changing the names of the main characters, of course, so Kayleigh became Katie and Sophie was obviously Sophia. These are just the highlights from my list of what I wanted to be – at one point I wanted to buy and sell houses in Greece, and then I wanted to design and sell lingerie. Let's not forget about the time I was sure I wanted to be an actress and auditioned for a role in *Skins*. There was also a summer where I was sure I could be a professional discus thrower. Clearly I have always been a dreamer. I would find a skill, or be told I was good at something and then go and research how it could be a job or a means to make a lot of money. Growing up in a working-class background with a single mum, I had always wanted to make money. It was my way of making my mum's life easier. All these different job roles were a part of my escape plan. Dreaming up different roles almost weekly was fun for me.

Then I came across June Sarpong, or aunty June as I lovingly call her. She was introduced to me as one of the presenters on *T4*, Channel 4's very successful attempt to reach the youth audience. *T4* came out on Saturday and Sunday mornings, with interviews and live performances in between shows like *Hollyoaks*, *The Simpsons* and *Scrubs*. My sister and I had a routine: Mum left for work at 6 a.m. and came back around noon, so we had a few hours of uninterrupted telly time, alongside making sure the house was clean for my mum's return. And there was June Sarpong, alongside Vernon Kay, on my television, a Black woman who wore lip glosses that resembled the ones I bought from the hair shop. So that was my next dream: I was going to be the next June Sarpong, a Black woman on television.

> There was June Sarpong, alongside Vernon Kay, on my television, a Black woman who wore lip glosses that resembled the ones I bought from the hair shop.

Then my teenage life moved into full gear and I stopped thinking of my future and, instead, I started worrying about the size of my boobs, my boyfriend and how I could sneak out without my mum finding out. And then Year 10 came along and I had to choose where I wanted to work for my two-week work experience. On the list of jobs, which included working at the local Debenhams and at the mechanics, was a role at *Sugar* magazine. Now, if you were a teenager in the 2000s, you know how elite *Sugar* magazine was, you will also know about the graduation from *Mizz* to *Sugar* to *Bliss* and then to *More!* magazine. I wanted the *Sugar* role and, thankfully, no one else could be bothered to travel from Essex to Central London, so I got it.

Those two weeks at *Sugar* magazine instigated the whole course of my career. I would wake up early, wear whatever version of smart-casual I had and then make my way to Marble Arch. Once I got to the station, I made a stop at Starbucks to buy a hot chocolate because I was entirely too immature to like the taste of coffee. With my hot chocolate in hand, I would walk into the *Sugar* magazine office. This was it, I thought, this was what life was meant to be. I had my own desk and I was around women who were well dressed and had shiny hair. The office had pictures of celebrities I had only dreamt of meeting and a beauty desk filled with every make-up brand I had seen at Superdrug. During my time there, I wanted to shine; I wanted to be the best work experience girl they'd ever had.

I remember one day the editor asked me to come into her office because she wanted advice. It was a teen magazine, I was a teenager, and therefore, I was an expert. She wanted me to start looking after the problem pages of the magazine; I was to read through the letters that had come in and pick the good issues. I quickly decided these problems were not good enough so I began making up dilemmas. My dilemmas were detailed and juicy. So, after passing her test, she invited me into her office again and said she wanted me to write an article for the magazine: an article where I was Paris Hilton for the day. It was the 2000s and Paris Hilton was the *It Girl*. The task involved me spending the day carrying a dog in my handbag. I have, and have always had, a huge fear of dogs, but I had decided that this was my time and I wanted to impress. That morning, I got to the office and I was introduced to Tolly the Dog – yes the dog was called Tolly, my childhood nickname. I had to carry the dog round in a little handbag and headed to Oxford Street with a photographer who was to pretend he was paparazzi.

We went into River Island and, somehow, convinced the manager that I was indeed a celebrity. Naturally, I spent the morning trying on outfits and chasing Tolly the Dog around the store. I got back into the office just after lunch and had to write my article which was shortly published, the first piece of work I ever had published. Once my two weeks ended, I was gifted with a box of goodies, a letter of recommendation and a solid decision of being a writer. And that was it, every choice I made after those two weeks was to help me become a writer at a magazine. I assumed every day as a writer would be as fun as my day spent with Tolly the Dog. I started spending a lot of my lunch money buying magazines and contacting the editors asking if I could do work experience. Upon writing this, I realise that it sounds like something out of *The Hills*.

I stayed consistent with my dream of being a writer and worked part-time jobs to make up for my unpaid work experience in journalism. My retail CV includes a role at Pizza Hut (which ended in me being fired after having a fight with the manager), H&M (which I left once COS opened across the street because I wanted to work in a posher environment) and then Santander (which I left once I got a full-time job at a magazine). Let me purposely leave out the days I spent trying to sell double glazing.

I don't have any secrets on how you can become a beauty journalist. I just applied for a lot of jobs and focused on the notion that I had to do better than good enough. I would often travel to the Blue Fin building, the home of IPC Media (now TI Media) and just fantasise about working there . . . it never happened. My career in journalism didn't have a sexy start. My first paid role was working as an intern for a magazine called *Fancy*, a magazine that was only available in Julian Graves, a store known for selling nuts. I was initially hired as a publishing intern, but I longed to work in editorial. So, when I overheard the editor of *Fancy* magazine, Julia Shaw, mention that she needed a taxidermist for a cover shoot, I stayed late that evening and found a place to hire the taxidermist, leaving the details on her desk. A week later, she asked if she could have me as her intern.

Julia took care of me, told me about the good old days of journalism and gave me so many chances. I was still at university when she hired me as her editorial assistant. I worked at *Fancy* for a year alongside my job at Santander. *Fancy* wasn't the dream actualised, it was just me writing about nuts, like actual nuts. I had an alliteration for every nut going. Clever cashews, amazing almonds, hazelnut heaven – I could go on for days. The closure of *Fancy* magazine was my first lesson in how unstable a career in the media can be. Julia was soon offered a new role as the editor of an over-60s magazine, *Life and Living*, and she took me with her. I would joke that the magazine should have been called 'Death and Dying' because I had to constantly deal with calls from family members who wanted to unsubscribe because the person had died. Then, history repeated itself and *Life and Living* closed. It was in the wake of its closure that I took on my first ever role as a beauty writer; a role Julia Shaw had recommended me for, where she left me in the arms of a new editor, Sofie West. It's important to me to mention the names of these women because both of them were so kind to me and spoiled me. In fact, they introduced me to a version of kindness that you don't get in all working spaces, especially as a Black woman.

> I noticed how my Blackness played a big role in my working life. I would often have to push to get Black beauty content written about.

As my career progressed, I noticed how my Blackness played a big role in my working life. I would often have to push to get Black beauty content written about. I'd have to force editors to see the importance of it and convince them that Black audiences should be targeted in lifestyle content – that they too should know what shade of red best suits their skin tone. The topic of my Blackness in the workspace wasn't just isolated to the mispronunciation of my name or microaggressions from white colleagues, it was also how I worked with other Black women in the workspace. Working with Black men was fine, I mean, I would have to deal with white colleagues suggesting we would make a good couple but that was OK. Meanwhile, working with Black women felt like competition. I would walk into a space, see the other Black girl in the office – because there was always only one other Black girl in the office – and I would instantly see her as competition. She wasn't a friend or a colleague, she was someone I felt I would be judged against. I did this based on how other Black women had treated me in past jobs. I don't know when I decided to stop this, and it might be thanks to a female empowerment brunch, but I did.

> I owe my whole career to Black women who I made friends with and Black women who made me their little sister.

This new mentality changed my whole working experience. The other Black girl in the office and I started exchanging compliments, as well as looks when someone said something racist. We went to lunch together and we took in the new Black women that joined the company. We formed a sisterhood, a sisterhood that has guided me ever since. I owe my whole career to Black women who I made friends with and Black women who made me their little sister; they encouraged me, while also telling me 'that ain't it, sis' with all the love in the world when they needed to. Black women who mentioned my name in rooms I had never entered. Everything I am is credited to the Black women who have loved me and I am so grateful for their friendship.

After years of working full-time and living my teenage dream as a writer, I got bored. Nothing excited me anymore and I found myself crying in the work toilets. Going freelance was not a conscious decision. I left my role at BuzzFeed out of frustration, I was over it all – I didn't have a big plan. I just wanted to see what would happen if I really took a chance on myself, if I learned new skills, really nurtured the podcast and wrote from my heart. What would my career look like then? This is what came out of it. Everything I am now is what came out of taking a chance on me.

My career now no longer fits into the description of work. I am lucky enough to have found purpose – a purpose and a paycheck. It's this sense of purpose that promises a future I am excited about but also a future I am little scared of. Really leaning into my purpose sees me fucking up the set – it taps into a dream so big, it takes my breath away.

✧

Audrey

I knew from a very young age that I wanted to do something creative. As a student, I worked really hard because it was the only way I knew how – I mainly did it because I wasn't naturally intelligent and didn't grasp things quickly. My motivation came from not wanting bad grades and never wanting to disappoint my parents.

Like most of my life, my career trajectory has been very linear. I was sixteen when I decided I needed to earn some coins honey and so I applied for a job at my local bakery, a small family-run business near my school. I bagged myself the job after an interview and, in true Audrey fashion, I gave it my all. The bakery was a pivotal moment for me because it was the first time I had independence – I was earning £4.80 an hour and it *was lit*. To this day, I can still make a great cup of tea and an amazing full English because of that job.

My time at the bakery was on and off for about seven years and, even at such a young age, I understood the importance of maintaining good relationships with my colleagues and managers. I worked hard, took on extra shifts and was great with customers. I also got free food so I was a happy bunny. Unfortunately, I also faced a few moral dilemmas at the bakery, including working with someone who was openly racist. My manager warned me before my first ever shift with her, pulling me into the back office and saying, 'I just wanna warn you about Sarah. She's a skinhead and I don't think she likes Black people.' Looking back, this is incredibly wild, but at the time, I didn't recognise how problematic it was – I was just grateful to have the job. I even saw it as a 'challenge' because I thought I could make her like me and, indeed, that's what I did. The woman I am today would never move like this and I'd probably try and take them to the cleaners but, back then, I genuinely didn't know any better.

I decided to level up and try and find a retail job because, by the time I was in university, I'd become a retail regular. I worked briefly in McDonald's and, when I say briefly, I worked there for a day. My shift was 7 a.m. to 11 p.m., I had to pay for my own uniform, and I had £20 taken out of my pay because I didn't have hard-soled shoes, by 10:30 a.m. I'd decided it wasn't for me. I also did stints at Nando's, Next, Aldo, Urban Outfitters and Tommy Hilfiger until I finally got the GOAT (greatest of all time, for the uninitiated) of all retail jobs. I'd applied for a job at Selfridges so many times and always got my application rejected but, finally, I found my way in through the back door when I got a job at Ted Baker and they told me they were moving me to the Selfridges Concession. Let me tell you, it felt good to be

God's favourite at that moment. Working in Selfridges was such a major part of my career journey because I made life-long friends and had the best time so it didn't feel like work. I'll never forget the memories we made, not to mention the celebrities I met including Kim Kardashian, Lenny Kravitz, Kelly Rowland and Jennifer Hudson.

After, I moved from Ted Baker to Levi's and there's one memory I'll always hold onto from my time there. One sunny Saturday morning, I was struggling to meet my target and was feeling a bit dejected on the shop floor when I clocked Noel Gallagher looking at some black Levi 501s. He came over to me for help and asked me why I looked so sad so I told him it was end of the week and I hadn't met target. He smiled and said 'Well, in that case, I'll take ten.' He spent a thousand pounds on jeans! I actually couldn't believe my luck. That's why I'll always maintain that Oasis are the greatest British band of all time. Thanks Noel, I'll never forget you.

Though I loved working in Selfridges for those five years, I eventually knew it was time to get serious about my career and think deeply about what I really wanted to do. And, though it might surprise you, my career of choice was to be a writer – more specifically, a celebrity or showbiz writer. I managed to blag an internship at *New!*, a showbiz magazine that was perfect because, even though it was unpaid, I was able to keep my role at Selfridges. I essentially worked Sunday to Sunday but I was young, hungry and loved every minute of it. I formed a great relationship with the staff and went on to intern there for a few years on and off, mainly stepping in when the Editorial Assistant was off or needed help. It was the first time I'd worked in a 9-5 office environment and it was so different to working in retail. My editor Kirsty was amazing and spurred me on so much. I came in early and left late, and though no task was beneath me, sadly this didn't manifest into a permanent job. That being said, it was so valuable in terms of learning and I got my first ever by-line thanks to that experience.

During my time there, I'd been applying for junior writer positions left, right and centre. It was deflating getting rejection after rejection, but people are right when they say it builds character. I remember vividly getting my fifteenth rejection of the week with the typical 'thanks for your application but unfortunately you don't have the relevant experience.' In the midst of frustration and rage, I replied, 'HOW AM I SUPPOSED TO GET EXPERIENCE IF YOU DON'T GIVE ME EXPERIENCE?' Don't do that, kids. One piece of advice I'd give to graduates on the job hunt is to remember that you're not alone – it's an anomaly to walk out of university and into your dream job. I know it will seem like everyone is winning but your journey will be different and individual – what is meant for you will be. Please do not be disheartened by rejection, it's an unfortunate part of life and we've all been through it.

I decided to apply for receptionist roles because of all this rejection – the strategy behind this was to get a well-paid admin job that wasn't too strenuous so I could continue applying for writer roles. My luck seemed like it was turning around when a junior writer position came up at *OK!* magazine, which happened to be under the same umbrella company as *New!* magazine. I used my connections and asked my now-former *New!* editor Kirsty to write a letter of recommendation to increase my chances of getting an interview and it worked. I was so incredibly gassed and overly confident. At the time, print journalism was still very much a thriving industry, so I collated all my published work into a folder and got ready for my interview. I was convinced that, not only had Kirsty's letter basically guaranteed me the job, but I had also killed the interview. I was presentable, charming and honestly left feeling so confident that I almost didn't go to an interview I had for a receptionist role that same day. I only went to the latter interview purely because I was already in central London. To my absolute shock, I didn't get the job at *OK!* magazine but I got the receptionist job. I couldn't even celebrate because I was so gutted. I think I cried for three days straight but I humbled myself and accepted the receptionist role which was at a luxury fashion and PR company.

I eventually got over the fact that I didn't get my dream job, dusted myself off and started my role at the PR company, which was a brand-new experience for me. I'm assuming you've seen *The Devil Wears Prada?* Well, that should give you an idea of what that job was like. In the end, I became so immersed in my role that applying for junior writer roles fell by the wayside. The office was plush, the clients were luxury and the staff were all middle-class white girls. I took ownership of my role and I did such a good job that the team referred to me as the face of the company. I knew all the clients by name and loved the fact I could get really dressed up every day. I had so many firsts, including working the *Elle* Style Awards and assisting on fashion shoots. The freebies were also plentiful.

As exciting as it was, it also came with hard times, including an incident where I felt I was bullied by one of the account executives. In my first week, she made my life hell but I kept my mouth shut because I was on probation and I didn't want to ruffle any feathers until I passed. She talked to me like shit, threw documents at me and demanded I did things for her that were out of my remit. She was racist but I also think she liked the power of finally having someone beneath her. I really needed the money and, for the most part, I was loving the job so I decided to firm it. To my surprise, however, my boss called me into his office one day to have a chat and said, 'I heard [insert name of bully here] has been giving you a hard time'. I didn't want to snitch but the opportunity was right in front of me so I took it. I told him what had been happening and his reply shocked me. 'Well, I want you to know that we don't tolerate bullying here so we've let her go,' he said.

I genuinely couldn't believe it but it felt good to have someone on my side and to not be gaslit. I realise this is almost unheard of, especially for young Black women in the office starting out, but, unfortunately, bullying in the workplace is pretty common. For anyone experiencing this I'd say the following:

* Keep track of the incidents, write them down to bring up later with HR. In other words, keep the receipts.

* Tell someone you trust so that you have witnesses. It'll be to your benefit in case you want to take things further. This way it isn't just your word versus theirs.

* Don't allow yourself to be a mule in the workplace and learn to say no. When people see you're eager to please they can take advantage. Show you're hardworking without being the office mug.

* Question microaggressions. Inappropriate questions about where you're *from* from, your hair or your culture are the usual suspects.

I was promoted to PA of the COO (the man who sacked the bully) and, though I've since moved companies, I've been a PA ever since. As you can see, my journalism dream never quite worked out for me but I think it's important to share wins but also failures. I continued to write the odd piece here and there but eventually, I stopped because it just became a constant reminder that I hadn't made it. I'm here to tell you that, sometimes, you don't make it and that's OK.

My journalism dream never quite worked out for me but I think it's important to share wins but also failures.

Audrey

We live in a time where it seems like everyone has multiple streams of income and side hustles. Yes, if you can monetise a hobby and have the capacity to do so, then you do you, but it's also OK to have a job that purely pays the bills and keep your hobby to a hobby – or even have no hobby at all. I wanted to be a journalist but, in my journey, I ended up doing something completely different. I believe all of these experiences have contributed to the path I'm on now. I think there are some careers that you fall into because you didn't even know it was a thing. I don't think any child thinks, you know what, I want to be a PA or I want to be a HR director, but you may end up there. A career is what you make it.

Doing PA work was never my goal but I made it work for me by ensuring I became a PA in a creative environment. I've had some super dope experiences shadowing senior people at very cool places, including AEG music, Burberry, Universal Music Group and Manchester United HQ. I've seen people get sacked and I've been influential in people getting second stage interviews so it's been fun.

I'm a podcaster but this is still something I struggle to claim. When people ask me what I do, I tend to stick to PA but I need to overcome that. Yes, I still have my full-time job and I love it. I think it keeps me grounded. I often get asked how I juggle both and the answer is being super organised, waking up early and trying to be as focused as possible. When the podcast first started, I never thought in a million years that I'd be writing a book off the back of it. I never thought we'd get paid to do it or have any of the mind-blowing opportunities we've had, yet here we are. As someone who found success with their hobby later on in life, I believe my journey is a testament to the fact that anything can happen if you believe you can do it and, even if you don't, you just never know what God has in store for you, so buckle up and enjoy the ride.

✧

Milena

I reckon my career journey started when I began singing from the age of five, doing up concerts in 'La Casa Del Frontroom' for my family. I wanted to have that spotlight whenever I could. I know they were all so tired of me, still are to be fair. As you can imagine, I was a very energetic child and the only way my aunty and uncle were able to keep me in one place for hours (and stop me pestering them) was by showing me the video recorder. They taught me how to connect it to the TV and I would spend my days filming myself for hours on end – I even did up outfit changes. I am still as grateful for that recorder now as I was back then because I am able to look back at my poor makeshift music videos and show Cataleya how I would spend my time when I was growing up. My love for the limelight wasn't confined to my living room. When I was a teenager, I took part in many Latin competitions and carnivals. I'd perform whenever I got the chance, a confident performer who loved showing off her talents. There was no way somebody was going to tell me that my name and face weren't going to be on billboards.

At the age of eighteen, I was discovered by the creator of *ChannelU*, Darren Platt (RIP), who arranged a meeting to see what we could do with my talents. This was when I met my manager, best friend and Cata's godfather, Colin Batsa. I had zero expectations going into this meeting – we started off with talking about placing me in a group that had already been created but I didn't want to feel like I was coming into something that was already formed. I suggested we make a completely new group. I remember Darren and Col looking at me as if I was mad but they went along with it anyway. Col had two guys in mind and before we knew it, the band, Code Red, was born (if you know, you know). Col must have thought his job was done after setting us up (*big* mistake) but I used to be on Col's line every day for about a month, *begging* him to manage me. I vividly remember one time when I was on lunch at my retail job and it was my fourth call to him. He wasn't picking up or responding to my messages but, eventually, he picked up and said, 'Milena, please, I'll call you after this meeting, stop calling me' to which I responded: 'Manage me then, let's sign a contract and I'll stop pestering you.' I guess being persistent worked in my favour because he recognised my hunger and decided he wanted to be part of my journey.

By this point, Code Red was now my new hope and focus. We spent nights in the studio working on our first single and then that's when 'Over' was born (yes, it's still on YouTube). We honestly didn't think anything of the song and thought that Col was going to *despise* it, but the moment he heard it, he looked at us and said, 'This is a hit'. We didn't believe him. Being an unknown group, we didn't expect much when we put it out. I don't know what kind of brujería my Tías (which means Aunt in Spanish) had been doing but we woke up to 50,000 views and hundreds of comments! The song would play all day on *ChannelU* and I would constantly be getting Facebook messages like 'Omg you've made it, I just saw you on my TV.' The song had been out for about a week when we performed at the *ChannelU* Xmas Bash at the O2 Indigo. We didn't think anybody would know the words, considering it had only been out for a matter of days, but when I tell you that these lot *sang every word back to us*, I was so overwhelmed. Hearing people sing your lyrics back to you is such an indescribable feeling. The funny thing was, the year before, I was at the same event when I met UK rapper Ghetts and I confidently told him I was a singer. He responded with 'Cool, on my set, I'm going to call you out, you on it?' I was shit scared, but I was always somebody that took opportunities and that's exactly what I did: I went out there, completely unknown, and I loved every moment of it. Who'd have thought that, 365 days later, I would not only be known but people would be asking me for pictures? Yeah, I was living the life. I met people on this part of my journey that now looking back, I think wow, you actually knew about me?!

After that specific show, I remember being outside the venue and some guy came up to us and said that we were really sick. He was a singer who had also performed that evening and we had a conversation, wished him the best and parted ways. That man was Ed Sheeran. But the fact that I was able to be in certain spaces, around such talent and also work with respected UK artists like Devlin, honestly made me believe I was on my way. So, understandably, when that was stripped from me one day during Code Red's UK tour, I was devastated. We split up and those of us left were all so confused, distraught and we just kept thinking, where do we go from here? I wanted to fight them of course, but I'm a child of God. We continued the group after finding a replacement but it wasn't the same. We ended up letting nature take its course and I continued as a solo artist with Col; he believed in me too much for me to just give up. I will always be grateful for that.

Going solo meant I had to put in extra work as I didn't get to share the pressure with two other people but I was OK with that. I think the hardest part of being a solo artist was that there was so much focus on me as an individual. I would constantly be reminded by people in the industry that I had to lose weight, as I was 'too big'. (Not by Col though, he always used to shut those comments down!) Now, looking back, mate, I wish I was that 'big' now. I ended up getting a trainer and working my little butt off, working on my stamina and image the best I could. Col had arranged an industry listening party for my album as a major label was interested in me so I wanted to look the part. But, in August 2014 – two months before this party – I fell pregnant. I remember the moment I saw 'pregnant 1-2 weeks' vividly and how my heart dropped. I was on contraception and

I had missed a couple pills but thought nothing of it. I had been with my boyfriend for six years and naturally, it was the next step for us. I'll admit it here: we weren't in the greatest place in our relationship and we thought having a baby would save us so for him, for us, I risked it all.

I was twenty-two and having a baby. You would think that this was the scariest part but, in reality, it was thinking about how I was going to break the news to Col. It ended up being one of the most daunting moments of my life. I walked into the Universal building, sat in a room and told him. He was shocked and I could see it though he never said it – he was disappointed. Being a manager is such a selfless job. He had invested so much into me, we had made big plans for the next few months and now, here I was, pregnant.

I felt awful. He supported me but naturally our friendship dynamic was shaken. Thankfully, we are now closer than ever and he is an amazing godfather to Cataleya. She loves her Coco so much and, no matter what, this man has

> The passion for music that I was born with had faded away and I was at my lowest.

always had faith in me. After I had Cataleya, I felt like that 'singer who never made it'. My confidence was through the floor and my self-esteem was like my dad – nowhere to be found. Feeling like a failure, I constantly questioned what I was going to do with my life; the passion for music that I was born with had faded away and I was at my lowest.

Career

I guess God had other plans. I remember a friend messaging me 'Yo, what's your email address? You was @d in a thread on Twitter about a podcast'. I wasn't on Twitter like that so I had no idea what he was talking about, nor was I into podcasts so I didn't think anything of it. Eventually, after a few meet-ups, drinks and discussions, we all made it happen. I fell into something that was therapeutic, something that could build my confidence and allow me to meet new women to share experiences, opinions and funny stories. Never in my wildest dreams did I think that this was going to be life-changing, that we would be on billboards, receive awards, be on the front page of magazines and have features in others. It was the recognition I had always dreamt of.

I've really enjoyed doing the podcast: I've met some amazing people, built a friendship with girls that were once strangers and had opportunities that I would never have imagined after having Cataleya. As much as it has been amazing, it has not been easy. I wouldn't be true to myself if I sat here without being honest. When I was younger, all I wanted was to be rich and famous. In my heart, I knew I was put on this earth for greatness but, on this journey, I have slightly lost myself. Sometimes I will go back and listen to old episodes and I feel like I was the most authentic version of myself back then: I was outspoken, I didn't care about what people would think, I never felt judged and whatever I felt, I said without thinking about fear. Though, naturally, I have grown and think a little bit more before I speak, I feel like I've lost that daring and energetic side to myself. This is mainly because, the bigger your platform becomes, the more your shit gets scrutinised; the more you are spoken about, the more people begin to feel like they know you better than yourself and that shit is hard. I feel like I've essentially had to filter myself and simmer down, but all I ever want is to be completely myself no matter what. It's hard when you feel like you will be judged if you aren't upholding certain standards and it's even harder when you feel like you can't put other things straight because you have to be the 'bigger person' or 'pay no mind' – especially because I've grown up acting like I'm on *Bad Girls Club*. There's a part of me that does not give a fuck about what people think but then there's another that feels like running into a room and never coming out. I'm

> I'm achieving those dreams I've had since forever, but at times, I feel like I've compromised my own mental health.

only human and a lot of the time, I'm battling more than people know and more than I can actually speak on. It's a bittersweet feeling because I'm achieving those dreams I've had since forever, but at times, I feel like I've compromised my own mental health.

This will be a shock to some because I seem so 'confident'. Though I am to a certain extent, my temporary (because I'm working on breaking off our relationship) anxiety has held me back a hell of a lot. You cannot see anxiety; it does not have a set way or structure on how or when it presents itself. Anxiety is unpredictable. Trying to control certain thoughts and managing the physical symptoms are the most mentally and physically draining things I've ever experienced but I get on with it. Anxiety doesn't work well under pressure or when I'm outside of my comfort zone, especially when doing interviews. Sometimes I'll feel OK and then other times I'll feel myself crumbling inside but I push myself because I know I am capable. Before, I used to work well on the spot. I could improvise and really had the gift of the gab but now, I find myself questioning whether what I'm saying even matters. As I talk, I question whether the words that are coming out of my mouth even make sense. More time, I say the bare minimum and let the girls talk to save myself the embarrassment if my mind decides to stop working. Despite the anxiety and judgement from others, there is no way that I can let these feelings and thoughts force me to give up on something I've worked so hard on; something that has really changed my life and brings me so much pride and happiness. My daughter and her future, alongside my growth, push me to work on my issues, like my anxiety, on a daily basis because I know this is not me forever (God, I am so grateful for my therapist!).

The thing that I love the most about doing this podcast are the live shows. I mean, I worry because you can't edit it, but I feel like I do my best when I'm on stage – there is this sense of home that I feel up there that probably harks back to where I started out. Though there are little voices in my head telling me all the things that could potentially go wrong, they are pushed aside when I see the listeners, interact with them, and hear them laugh – it's a beautiful feeling. It reminds me of the community we have essentially built and how I would hate to no longer be a part of it. The messages we receive, as a collective and individually, make me realise how much of an impact we've had on people's lives. Digesting the magnitude of appreciation that we receive reminds me that there are people out there who aren't out to get you or criticise you. It has been especially helpful for me when there are people that have openly related to me and it has helped me feel less alone, especially during the 2020 pandemic.

Talking about feeling less alone, music has never really left me and will always be my first love. I've been recording, writing and creating silently in the background because I really didn't want to commit to anything publicly – I knew that that bitch anxiety would have me wanting to scrap all the hard work because of fear. But the more I record and get feedback, the more I know my stuff is worth being out there. I want to do music because I love it, because it is my passion and because, as much as I love talking about all the shit

> My daughter and her future, alongside my growth, push me to work on my issues, like my anxiety, on a daily basis because I know this is not me forever.

I've been through, I would love to sing about it too. However, I want to do it at my own pace. Regardless, I cannot wait, I am excited and I will not allow my thoughts to get

Career

the best of me – I deserve to be heard in all mediums. If you are reading this and you've stopped doing something you love because of anxiety, fear, worry or because your dumb ex said some madness to you, please pick it up and start again. You can do it.

✧

A Woman Who Inspires
Audrey

The incredible women who have surrounded me in my life have shaped me into who I am. Whether they be family, friends or colleagues, it's women who have helped me navigate my way through life with ease, compassion and tenacity. I come from a line of strong women who, through it all, manage to enjoy themselves, laugh unapologetically, look amazing and thrive despite the odds being stacked against them. I knew I wanted to write about someone in my family because we rarely get a chance to give flowers to the people who've inspired us. Everyone mentioned in this book has had an impact on me but, specifically, it's my aunt, Salome Muno, who I wanted to write about here – although it's weird calling her that because she's more like a cool older cousin.

Salome is my mum's first cousin and really is one of the most fabulous women on the planet. I still vividly remember her babysitting me when I was a little girl; she would've been a teenager at the time. We'd go swimming, she'd take me to school and I always thought she was the coolest person – it was kind of like having a big sister. One of my fondest memories is of watching her and her best friend get ready to go to the bar, Ace of Clubs in East London's Forest Gate, back in the day. She won't know this but, when she was out, I'd sneak into her room and try on her clothes and shoes – I might have even stolen a scarf in the mid-nineties. When I messaged Salome and asked to interview her for the book, she called me straight away close to tears and, there and then, I knew I'd chosen the right person.

Salome has been inspiring me since I was a child. She carries herself with poise and class at all times, she has the most elite style, has two fabulous daughters and she has also carved out a successful career in fashion. I can't imagine what trials and tribulations she would've faced as a visible Black face in an already intense and cut-throat industry, and I wanted to know more about her experiences.

✧

AUDREY: What were you like as a little girl?

SALOME: I had a *vivid* imagination. I used to write short stories. I was also convinced I would be a famous author and fashion designer. The little girl inside me still secretly desires an author's life.

A: When did you decide you wanted to go into fashion?

S: Growing up, I was surrounded by many family fashion icons. My mum, my aunties and many of my cousins were so stylish and, in the eighties, you were never fully dressed without matching shoes and bags. I remember watching *Dallas* and *Dynasty* with my family but most of the time we didn't even pay attention to the juicy plots – it was always the outfits that shone the most!

It was a natural progression for my creativity. The task was convincing my parents, away from the expected lawyer or doctor roles. I think many of us can relate to this, especially if you grew up with strict African parents. The concept of doing something creative was almost disrespectful. Though I didn't understand this at the time, as I've gotten older, I get it more. A lot of our parents came here with very little and managed to carve out lives for themselves doing menial jobs or learning a skill to ensure they'd always be able to earn. The pressure for us to be in high-flying positions stems from fear. They want us to be in secure and stable careers because, in their eyes, that is the highest of heights.

A: As first-generation children of immigrants, we have the privilege to be able to see all of the options available to us, so this just speaks volumes about your tenacity and bravery to go against a strict African mother and pursue your passions. After gaining a better understanding of what you wanted to do, I want to ask, were you ever discouraged to focus on your career because you're a woman?

S: Never. I come from a family of many matriarchs. My mum was a NHS nurse and businesswoman with a property portfolio in the UK, Africa and the Caribbean. She had a 'work hard' ethos but, equally, knew how to enjoy herself and would travel for shopping trips and holidays all over the world. I wanted that life so I knew I had to work hard for it too.

A: We absolutely do come from a family of strong women and I think this will be passed down for generations to come. Having had a brief stint in fashion myself . . . OK OK, I was on reception, but I technically still worked at a fashion PR company! However, even at a junior level there, I dealt with racism and microaggressions. I'd like to know what that looks like when you're more senior? What obstacles have you faced as a Black woman in your field?

S: Fortunately, the editorial fashion world had a very strong female presence when I started. Most of the respected fashion editors were female and fierce too! My mentor and dear friend, Jenny Asiama – then Deputy Fashion Editor of *The Sunday Times* – plus other strong female Fashion Directors like Karen Binns and the late Isabella Blow, just to name a few, helped me feel empowered.

Regarding racism, I've been in this industry for nearly twenty-five years, so I have had my share of experiences. Often, I was the only Black woman in the Fashion departments I worked in. However, growing up in the seventies and eighties in the East End to a working-class divorced mum instilled a strength in me that I often tapped into when racism reared its ugly head. I remember one occasion when I was Style Editor for *The Times* Saturday paper. I had been invited to a high-end launch. The PR and I had been liaising most of the day and she had arranged my arrival to the VIP event. When I arrived at the agreed meeting place, she walked past me and I saw her ask a security guard to question me, not realising she had invited me. The shock on her face when she realised was a picture! She didn't expect a Black woman to be in such a prestigious role or hold that title. Needless to say, I did not stay.

A: Hearing this story makes me realise how sadly things haven't changed. Black women are still being questioned about their positions, even when they're more senior and more qualified.

Aside from carving out an amazing career in fashion and being the former style editor at *The Times*, *The Daily Express* and FashionSOS.co.uk, you are also the mother to two amazing daughters and you also care for your mum. In a climate where we ask if women can really have it all, I want to pick your brain on motherhood and your career.

S: The juggle is real! Being a mum to my two beautiful girls (Sahara is eighteen and has a disability and Tia is eight) on top of being a carer for my amazing mum who lives with us has its challenges, but I have a fantastic team of carers, and a wonderful housekeeper to help out. Plus, with the love and support of my friends and family, I'm able to make it work. I've worked really hard for my career and love what I do, so I am a firm believer in having to all.

A: And so you should! I also want to know what the hardest part of your career has been so far?

S: In the early days of my career, it was dealing with *The Devil Wears Prada* types! It fed into my imposter syndrome and so it took a while for me to believe in myself.

A: Whew, relatable. So what's the best and hardest part about being a mother?

S: The best has to be the overwhelming and unconditional love I have for my girls. Being a mother also extends to my other babies: my step-sons, godchildren and friends' children who I have been blessed with along the way. It takes a village! The hardest part is the 'mum guilt' that still stings when you least expect it. Even now, as a freelancer with a much better work/life balance, I am still haunted by second-guessing my parenting when I know I have made the best choices.

A: It's so important to hear about the balance between being a career woman and mother in the modern world, and to share these stories of women who have overcome obstacles to really have it all. Finally, I want to know about legacy, what do you want yours to be?

S: Gosh, that's the ultimate question! I have had many life experiences. Ultimately, I would like my legacy to be my strong, resilient daughters and that they will grow to be their authentic selves, always knowing they *are* good enough and continue to conquer their dreams.

✧

Tolly

It's 18 November 2020. Having received the keys to my house days before, I'm in the middle of stripping pink ballerina wallpaper off the wall of a bedroom that once belonged to one-year-old triplets. Then I get the call: my dad has died. My brother, his firstborn, announces it on the phone matter-of-factly. 'Dad said he wasn't feeling well. He went upstairs to rest and he was found on the floor sweating, taken to hospital and then pronounced dead,' he tells me. His death was sudden, my dad wasn't sick, he had in fact sent me his daily chain message that morning, which I'd ignored.

My dad's death is more integral to my life than I would like to admit; it was in his death that I realised how much I craved him. How I longed to feel loved by him and how many of my fantasies included a version of him. His death also brought up many questions, questions that I will now never get answers to. I wondered what it would be like to have grown up with him. I considered what type of woman I would be if he was around all the time or even just the times that I needed him to fix something. But death strips that away from you; it shouts your questions into an empty void that will never answer back.

At its best, death allows you to see a person in a different light. For all of its grief and pain, death allows you to connect with the people the dead left behind. I am comforted by the stories of people who knew him, the people he made feel good. However, at its worst, death leaves you with anger, a rage that bubbles up inside, one that comes and goes and then comes back again. Although anger is a fleeting emotion, it is one I found myself trying to latch on to. It allowed me to make sense of things. Of course I was angry: my dad was dead and any chance of us having a healthy relationship went with him. But there was something about watching his body get lowered into the ground that made my anger feel silly. It was in that moment of finality that I knew I could no longer hold on to this anger. The anger wasn't going to give me comfort and, instead, forgiveness had to show up. But forgiving someone who can't show remorse or make amends is hard. For me forgiveness has always gone hand in hand with someone changing – how can the dead change?

> Death shouts your questions into an empty void that will never answer back.

Forgiving my dad and allowing myself to love him is a process. Some days, I am sure I have grasped it, while on others, the anger and resentment show up. In spite of it all, I hold on tightly to the fact that I know my dad loved me. He told me this often, I just wish I felt it. The issue with my dad's love is that I have my mum's love to compare it to. My mum's love wraps its arms around me; it cuddles me, and even when it feels suffocating, it is still good.

✧

My mum's love for my siblings and me existed before we even knew it. She migrated from Lagos, Nigeria, in 1988, leaving two children behind. After a year in the UK, I was born – my dad was a pilot so he left her with the gift on a stopover trip. London was a promise of a better life for her children. She left her home, her friends and came to a country where she didn't speak the language, a country that quickly showed her that it reserved its kindness and privileges for its own. A sacrifice I don't think I would be able to make. I lived in London for a year before she took me to Nigeria. Raising me alone in a country that was foreign to her, a place where she didn't have a village, proved too difficult. With all her kids in Nigeria, my mum returned to England and started learning how to navigate life in

> My mum left her home, her friends and came to a country where she didn't speak the language, a country that quickly showed her that it reserved its kindness and privileges for its own.

London, she made new friends and worked multiple jobs to gather money together to bring my sisters and me to England. I had been told that she visited when I lived in Nigeria, but those stories are not mine. I have the clearest memory of seeing her for the first time. She was walking towards me and my sisters at London Heathrow airport and I knew it was her, not because I remembered her face, but because I saw my face in hers. I also knew from the way she came towards us, I felt like I saw love.

My features are not the only thing I share with my mum. I am like her in so many ways and we share many characteristics, including a simultaneous distrust and adoration for love. My mum has taught me so many things that have stuck to my insides like gum, some I am happy to leave an imprint, while others, I am learning to peel off. My mum wears all of the best bits of being a Yoruba woman – she has this 'Mo Ti De' (I have arrived) vibe when she walks into a room. It's the power and authority she naturally oozes. She is kind and my sisters and I lived in a household that was open to everyone who needed it. She taught us warmth, resilience and strength. So much of my best bits are a result of who my mum is and how she brought us up.

I love my mum, but we don't have the perfect relationship – I don't know a mum and daughter duo that does. You see, even though my mum agrees that I am the protagonist in my own life, she continually tries to be the writer. And, as it turns out, her writing skills lean too much into her fears.

It was her fear of an unkind England that told us that we had to work twice as hard. It was her fear of shame that made sure we feared sex and stayed 'good girls'. And it's her fear of me doing life alone that makes her continually pressure me into finding a husband. My mum has always wanted us to have all the things she didn't; she craves a full life for us. And, with all of her sacrifices and how she dimmed her own light in order for her children to shine, the only way we can thank our mum is by shining so bright that she gets to bask in our light too.

I am the youngest of all my siblings, with a brother and sister from my dad, a sister from my mum and another sister, Dami, who I share my mum and dad with. My siblings have been generous enough to let me play out all the tropes that come with being the youngest, but there's something very special about Dami's generosity. Dami feels like she is mine and my favourite title is Dami's little sister. We share the same stories and she fills in my missing gaps. My most precious memories have her in them. I don't know life without my sister Dami. My other siblings have always felt like visitors in my life; visitors I love and welcome but not the type I let come round if the house is a mess. However, Dami not only comes when the house is a mess, she helps to clean it up. My dad's death changed my relationship with my siblings. It was after his death that I was able to tell my brother I loved him and felt warmth run through my body when he said it back. The language in my family has changed and conversations now end with 'love you'. We all have a longing to be around each other, to live a life that makes each other feel good. We feel like a team now.

My family portrait is one that needs a huge frame, my immediate circle is not limited to mum, dad and siblings. It's nieces and nephews, it's cousins, it's big mummies, it's aunts and uncles, and aunts and uncles that are not really aunts and uncles. We range in age and some of us don't really know each other. I am from the type of family that saw me being a bridesmaid for a second cousin who I had never met prior to her wedding.

My family is led by women; it's a kingdom where women rule and men have never really been the boss. Yes, the men are admired and respected, I mean, my little nephew gets the offering of two meats with his food, but they are never really the boss. These women were the first to love me; they taught me from early on how to manoeuvre in life, knowing I have them by my side. No one dealt with anything alone. Even when it felt lonely, you were never alone – you always had a group of women to help. My mum had aunties, both real and fake, to help look after us. They would take it in turns, so each other could work. They would put money together to take us on holidays and, even though these holidays didn't see us at airports, there wasn't a year where we didn't go to Butlin's or, at the very least, enjoy a day at the beach.

My family allowed me to see so many different variations of women. I had an aunty for everything and, of all the traditions of the Black family, aunties remain a staple. I can't write about my family without giving an ode to my aunties.

✧

My favourite aunty

The kindest of the whole bunch, there's not a birthday she forgets or a special occasion she doesn't show up for. She constantly checks in on me and makes food that competes with my mum's. She encourages me and softly corrects me.

My rich aunty

You see, my rich aunty is not necessarily the one who has the most money, but she sure is the flashiest. She wore designers before I knew how to pronounce them. She manages to look rich without ever looking like she has worked a day in her life.

My aunty who is sure she still has it

Every conversation with this aunty starts with 'awon girls'. She is sure she doesn't look a day over 30, but everything about her says otherwise. She still lives off the high of her heydays, or 'ayyyyee days' as she now refers to them.

The witch-adjacent aunty

The shadiest of them all, she knows the gossip about everyone and, anything she doesn't know, she makes up. Even her compliments are laced with insults and she is the leader of the 'When will you marry?' gang. She manages to mention my singleness in every conversation, while not being in a relationship herself. She is entertaining until her attention is turned to me.

The cool successful aunty

This is the aunty that I long to be. The youngest of all the aunties, she has had the privilege of doing all the things she hoped for and more. She is the aunt that gives me the much-needed pep talk, the one that reminds me to not measure my life according to society or cultural expectations.

Family

The 'Big Mummy' aunty

The aunties who we lovingly call 'Big Mummy' are older than all the other aunties, in fact, this kind of aunty helped raise all the other aunties. She is the head-aunty-in-command. I don't just have one Big Mummy in my life – they are scattered around the globe. From Big Mummy America, to an aunt with so much authority, she skipped the 'Big Mummy' title and jumped to 'Grandma Canning Town'. It was 'Grandma Canning Town' who introduced me to Jerry Springer. She would watch the show, while chanting *'Jerry! Jerry! Jerry!'* at the screen.

✦

My favourite moments are when all my aunties are together, they share a joy that is contagious, a joy that is in the very fabric of what makes my family.

Audrey

Family for me has always been something very insular, consisting of my mum, dad, brother, sister and maternal grandmother. My parents met as teenagers in Ghana and have been together ever since. As I got older, I realised that it wasn't necessarily the most conventional marriage by Western standards but a very typical African set up, as from around 2010, my dad would travel back and forth from England to Ghana.

My earliest memories consist mostly of my wider family on my mum's side; aunts, uncles and cousins. There was rarely a holiday where we weren't all together celebrating something, usually meeting at my aunt Rose's house, my grandmother's sister. She's what I'd describe as the matriarch of the family and was one of the first people in the family to migrate to England and build a great life for herself here. I'll never forget when the family would get together (which we'd create any excuse to do, including for the opening of a bottle of Supermalt) and watch Michael Jackson music videos. Everyone who knows me knows that I'm a Michael Jackson *stan* and I've always been. It was at one of these get-togethers that we watched the debut of *Remember the Time* and I cried from joy and happiness. Being surrounded by all my loved ones while enjoying my favourite artist was such a pure and untainted version of happiness, it filled me up 'til it spilled over.

✧

I've been lucky enough to always have a beautiful relationship with my mum, Angelina. We're very different personality-wise but, as a child, I was a complete Mummy's Girl. For the first few years of my life, it was just my mum and me, so I remember moments when we were together with clarity. My parents lived separately when I was a baby but then reunited and got married when I was about five. As a little girl, I idolised her. I thought, and still think, that she's the most beautiful woman on the planet. I'd look up at her and say, 'Mummy, you're so pretty' and she'd always reply with, 'You too, darling.'

When I think about what my mum managed to achieve as a Black African woman who came to this country in the eighties, I feel so proud. I can only imagine what she went through and the strength and tenacity she would have needed to get through her toughest times. She has shared many stories about things that happened to her and my grandmother when they came to England and, if I'm honest, I don't think I could have handled it. One thing I've tried to do as I've gotten older is not to attribute strength to the Black women in my life. I've seen how damaging this trope is because it creates this illusion that we can innately endure more and, therefore, aren't worthy of protection. I've always viewed my mum as a strong woman but now, I can think of so many moments where she was probably crumbling inside.

> I've always viewed my mum as a strong woman but now, I can think of so many moments where she was probably crumbling inside.

My mum always worked hard. I remember her doing a secretarial course, where she learned short-hand, and being so impressed by how fast she could type. She initially came to this country to train as a nurse but when she found out she was pregnant with me, that dream was put on hold for many years. However, in true Angelina fashion, she got back on the horse when my brother was a toddler and eventually qualified as a nurse, and later, as a midwife. My mum had an amazing balance of being firm and fair and I want to adopt her style of parenting when I become a mother one day. Even to this day, I care majorly about what my mum thinks and I can't let an argument fester with her.

I consider myself so privileged to still have my mum alive and well, so I cherish our relationship very much. With that being said, I think there comes a time with all mother-daughter relationships where there's a natural clash and this happened in my mid-twenties. I think there's some-thing about two women living in a household together where you really have to find a way to navigate around each other. As you get older, you have to find a balance between 'I'm a woman now and you will respect me' and the reality of still living under your parent's roof – which happens more and more as housing prices and renting becomes increasingly expensive – and this was a struggle for my mum and me for a couple of years. Being raised in a family where there was very little privacy and everything was out in the open was a hard adjustment for my mum to make. I had gone from being a little girl and teenager who told her everything to suddenly being a woman with my own life and secrets, and it definitely impacted our relationship. She couldn't understand why I didn't want to tell her every little thing about my life but, after many explanations and arguments, she started to ease off. The beautiful thing about my relationship with my mum now is that she fully respects me, not only as her daughter, but as a woman. She's learned to take constructive criticism and often comes to me for advice, which honestly melts my heart.

My mum would say her number one achievement in this life is her kids and I really believe that. This is one of the reasons she's desperate for me to become a mum; she worries that I won't have that experience and it terrifies her. By the time she was my age – I'll be thirty-five when this is published – she'd had all three of her children, so she can't fathom the fact that I haven't had a baby yet. I know there are a lot of women out there also facing this pressure from family. I have to remind her that times are different now and, even though it's something I really want, she has to be at peace with the fact that it may not happen. This is probably the biggest educational lesson I've given my mum: that there isn't one set way to live life and it's so important to respect people's choices, especially when it comes to family. She's from a different generation and, to add to the equation, she's an African woman, so the concept of doing anything remotely unconventional scares the shit out of her. Just like so many other mums, in her mind, you get married, have kids and everything else comes after. Don't get me wrong, she's so proud of everything I've accomplished and she makes a point of letting me know that, but making her a grandmother is her biggest dream of all. I'm not going to lie, the pressure feels immense sometimes, especially when approval from my mother means everything to me. Though I won't be pressured into a life that isn't meant for me, I really hope I can make that dream come true for both of us.

> There isn't one set way to live life and it's so important to respect people's choices, especially when it comes to family.

✧

My dad is a very special human being and I feel so lucky to have the relationship I have with him. When my dad heard I was born, he gave up his dreams and passions in Ghana to come to cold and rainy England so he could be a part of my life. My parents didn't get back together instantly, so I vaguely remember moments where I'd go and spend the weekend with him while he was living with my aunt in North London. There's a picture of me sitting on his lap crying my eyes out, probably because I wanted my mum!

Once my mum and dad figured it out, we lived as a family of four until my sister was born. I've said this before on the podcast, but I legitimately do not remember being poor – I always felt like I had it all as a child. My dad worked so hard; he's told me a lot about the jobs he had in the past but the job that stands out to me the most was his role as a caretaker at what later became my secondary school. It holds a special place in my heart because my primary school was down the road and sometimes my dad would pick me up after school and I'd wait for him to finish work there. I vividly remember running up and down the halls thinking how huge the building looked to me. I can still remember the smell of the buffering machine. My dad is one hell of a guy, honestly the nicest man you'll ever meet. He's kind, warm and just so cool. I've never ever felt embarrassed by either of my parents (probably because they're so young) but my dad is the one who really oozes cool. The majority of my family on my dad's side have always lived in Ghana and, although he has a lot of friends and family in London, I think his heart has always stayed in Ghana. I think if he could've had it his way, he would've raised us there, so as amazing and present as my dad is, I think there's always been a slight regret within him, wondering about what could've been had he not migrated to England. I never felt that as a child but, looking through an adult lens, I see it now.

✦

In my household, my mum was the disciplinarian which I think is common in a lot of Ghanaian homes. My dad rarely disciplined us unless he had to. I was generally a good kid – OK, OK, a geek – so I was rarely smacked by either parent, but there was one occasion where I needed my dad to sign a consent letter for me to attend a trip to Thorpe Park. He said he would sign it and leave it on the dresser, but that wasn't good enough for me, so I went downstairs three or four times urging him to sign it. He smacked me on the legs and I didn't ask him to sign it again. Though, after a long restless night, I woke up to find the permission slip on my dresser, signed. I guess I remember it so clearly because it was the only time my dad smacked me. Having experienced a strained relationship with his own father, my dad made sure to spend time with us and he talked to us like grown-ups from early on. He even used to give us the tea on family secrets. He's also incredibly tactile, especially with my brother, which I love but, to be honest, he was so happy to have a boy after being outnumbered for so many years.

My dad doesn't conform to the stereotypes of a typical African man in the sense that he's incredibly domesticated. He's very organised and obsessed with cleanliness and, as a trained chef, can cook up a storm. Every Saturday, he'd play reggae music, open every window and deep-clean the whole house, also making sure that everything in his wardrobe was pressed to perfection and colour-coordinated. I never grew up seeing gender roles in any traditional sense because my dad was hands-on and always pulled his weight around the house. I think this is why I'm quite relaxed about splitting bills and going 50/50 with someone – I saw that in my parents my whole life.

✧

Being the eldest of three, I describe myself as a guinea pig because I had no one to ask for advice and had to figure things out on my own. That's why my brother and sister are so cool – they had me to guide them; I walked so they could run! I was able to give them tips on what to do and what not to do and they learned from many of my mistakes. One of those mistakes being that you definitely shouldn't opt for the school merch as your book bag, it's not cool.

For me, having a sister has been like having a built-in best friend and I'm so grateful for the relationship we have. My sister, Vanessa, is three years younger but definitely the more mature out of the two of us. When we were little girls, I really took my role as Big Sister seriously, which basically means that she was my very own personal assistant. She'd follow me around everywhere and she was my wingman when I was too scared to ask my parents for McDonald's. As sisters, we were raised to be close, sharing a room for most of our lives, and I'm so glad we've maintained our relationship because we wanted to, not because we had to. The most rewarding feeling is having someone who loves you unconditionally and who can provide a unique perspective because you grew up together. However, outside of being sisters, I realised recently that being close is actually a choice because I genuinely like who my sister is as a person. I just know I'd choose her as a friend.

I knew my sister was a real one when she stood up for me against a bully. I was twelve, so she would've been nine years old at the time. I made friends with the most popular girl on the estate called Chloe. All the boys fancied her, all the girls wanted to be her, and she always had the best tracksuits and trainers. We were best friends for all of a week before she ditched me out of the blue. I was absolutely gutted because, when you're a pre-teen, all you care about is acceptance. I later found out that her actual bestie was just on holiday and I was basically a fill-in. We saw her at the park and my sister approached her and said, 'You used my sister! She was good enough to be your friend when Charlotte wasn't here, what's that about?' Chloe looked at her and said, 'Used her? What am I her boyfriend or summink?' At the time, I was fuming that Vanessa did that. I was so concerned about being liked and not treading on toes that I didn't even realise that my sister was defending my honour in that moment. As a grown-up, I look back and can't believe how real and loyal she was, even at such a young age.

I can't remember the exact moment I went from having a 'little sister' to just having a sister. Age is such a thing in

African cultures that you can be just a few months older, but with age and respect being so closely tied, you have to behave accordingly. However, realistically, a three-year age gap is nothing and there comes a time when the power dynamic shifts. You relinquish your big sister powers and start to accept that person for who they are. It went from being forced to take my little sister everywhere with me to asking her to go out with me, the same way you'd ask a mate. Vanessa is the funniest woman on the planet. If anyone can make me belly laugh, it's my sister and to see her shine makes me so happy. Even though she's younger, my sister inspires me daily, especially as she has been through an abusive relationship and struggles in her career, but she has come back from those better than ever and her next relationship was with the nicest guy.

I have such a close bond with my sister that many people say to me that they didn't know I had a brother. Well, I do and he's the baby of the family. He's eight years my junior so I remember when he was born and the excitement that my parents were going to have a son. When Jake was a toddler, he was so vivacious, energetic and completely obsessed with Batman and Spiderman – he'd scream the house down if he had to take off his costumes. My mum and dad would have to ensure one was always clean so he could rotate them, *that's* how bad it was. Watching him grow into the man he's becoming now makes me so proud. There's always been a special place in my heart for my brother because I understand the pressures he may have felt to perform, especially as my sister and I were both quite studious.

Audrey

As my brother was becoming a teenager my mum was concerned about him because my dad was spending more time in Ghana and I think she worried he'd be led astray. Raising a young Black man in London is not easy and part of the reason my parents were adamant about moving from my estate was so he didn't fall in with the wrong crowd. My brother is very much an independent thinker and he never brought any trouble to my mum's doorstep, which speaks volumes. Like most young men, he keeps himself to himself, but I've always made it a point to let him know I've got him. On my wedding day, I remember him coming to my dressing room in his suit and tie and I burst into tears. I just felt so proud and he continues to make me proud. I'll never understand what it's like to live in a Black male body, so I think I overcompensate by spoiling my brother and throwing money at all his problems. For example, he's entrepreneurial and has a clothing line which he's executed and launched all by himself. When I offer to help him financially, he always tells me no and you know what? I get it and I rate it. I can't wait to see what my brother contributes to the world because I already know it's going to be magic.

Anyone who knows me knows how much my brother and sister mean to me. I mean it when I say their happiness is more important than my own. I know many aren't lucky to have as full a family as this but choosing your family can be just as powerful as blood relations. One thing I've learned over the years is while blood makes you related, loyalty makes you family. However, having both truly makes you privileged.

Milena

I regard a whole mixture of people as my family: some of us are blood related and some are friends that turned into family. At the end of the day, I love them all the same – even though some of them drive me crazy. The saying 'it takes a village to raise a child' couldn't be truer for me, I was raised by so many amazing individuals that all contributed to making me the woman I am today.

My mum came over from Colombia with my aunty Mia in the 90s, already pregnant with me at twenty-two. She didn't know the language and had no money. She was only meant to stay for six months but she eventually overstayed her welcome and spent many years as an illegal immigrant. This led to her moving out of my tia's home and leaving me with her. This was the best thing to do in her mind as, if she ever got caught, at least I had some stability with my living arrangements. I only discovered this a couple of years back and for a very long time, I felt like she had abandoned me just like my dad.

I held on to a lot of resentment towards them, especially once I became a mother myself, as I couldn't comprehend how a mum could leave her child. My resentment subsided when I took the time to watch old video recordings and look at photo albums at my tia's, coming to the realisation that my mum was actually there with me every day until I was around five or six. She loved me, she took care of me and she'd make me dance and sing in front of the camera while hyping me up. I wondered why, in my head, I had blocked all of this out? As a six-year-old child, not waking up to either parent every day felt like neglect. Unfortunately for me, that's what my lack of self-esteem was born out of.

Throughout my life, I have stuck to people like gum if they showed me just a little piece of love or affection. I did this because I always felt at some point that they would just up and leave me and that was incredibly hard to unlearn. I love my mum, I do, but our turbulent relationship is extreme. We are either so sweet with each other, or literally screaming at one another, it is *draining*. Many people from traditional households can probably relate to this but my mum doesn't like taking accountability and that response can feel like there's no point in having the conversation, so all the feelings stay pent up inside. This can be especially damaging when the build-up of emotions turn into resentment and anger, leading to a toxic or distant relationship. Sometimes I do feel bad about the way our relationship is and I always try to remind myself that she hasn't had it easy.

Family

You see, my mum was adopted, and not the typical sort of adoption where contracts are signed and a file of information is held if you ever wanted to trace your birth parents and so on. Instead, my mum was left outside a church in Medellín, Colombia, in a basket, very clearly premature and barely alive. My adoptive grandmother was a woman that would always be in church, she had thirteen kids (I know right) but her thirteenth child, who was a little seven-month-old girl, sadly passed away. The priest knew my grandmother and her situation well, so he asked if she would take in my mum. After arguing with my granddad, who didn't want another baby, my grandma took my mum in as her own. My tia, Mia, always tells me how the family thought she wasn't going to survive, considering how *tiny* my mum was when they first saw her. As time went on, my mum got stronger and stronger and became well-instated as the youngest of the household. Mum always felt like an outsider compared to her siblings; they all looked alike while she had a very different hair texture and facial features. In her mind, she felt she didn't belong and that she was the runt of the litter. Thankfully, my aunty always made sure to look after my mum and make her feel loved, long after my grandparents passed away.

So, when my mum and I argue and shout at each other, I feel so guilty afterwards. I get mad thinking about how she had three kids that needed a sense of stability and normality; one she just didn't provide, despite us being her only blood relatives. Then I come to realise that she never had that stability herself, so how could she give it to us?

Milena

This ping-pong battle I have in my head constantly goes back and forth with her and, though it's toxic at times, I do love her dearly. Aside from being a mum, she is a great time and a good friend to others so I've learned to accept her for what she is. I hope one day, we can go on a quest to find her real parents or family so she can find some peace in her heart.

✧

I was a huge rebel throughout my teen years and I couldn't be told by anyone. Well, that's what I thought until I met Simone, my baby dad's mum and Cataleya's grandma. I remember always being kicked out of my house due to the arguments my mum and I would have. It was an incredibly unstable environment and so Simone, who I call Madre, asked me to move in. She embraced me like the daughter she never had, but that also meant I wasn't getting away with anything. She treated me like one of her boys and she was just as hard on me as she was on them. That was a household where there was love, yet discipline. I remember one time (which I thought was my last day living and I know she remembers this too), I had failed my driving test and I walked into the house huffing and puffing, slamming doors. I heard her say to Kyle that even though I was upset I needed to respect the house. I was so angry and frustrated that I had failed, I fully lost my mind and went to confront her. I went to raise my voice, but my voicebox pretty much stopped working when I saw the way she looked at me. I felt the fear take over my body, but I still tried to proceed with my madness. She just stopped me and said, 'Don't you dare' in a way that meant that was the first and last time I ever tried it with her. We laugh about it now but, damn, I was shitting myself. It's what I needed though. I needed that tough love, that real love, that you-need-to grow-up-and-be-mature kind of love and Madre always gave me that. Even up until now, we annoy each other but we love one another to bits. We are super close and I know I can rely on her for advice on life.

> I needed that tough love, that real love, that you-need-to grow-up-and-be-mature kind of love.

✦

Now on to my sister, Andrea. My broke best friend and my first daughter. We have ten years between us but this bitch is the pen to my paper, even if I wasn't initially thrilled at the announcement of her existence. I was ten, living at my tia's house with my two cousins, Alex and Bridie, who I considered my siblings. I was the youngest and a spoilt brat so, when I found out that there would be someone who was going to push me off my little high horse, I was livid. I wanted to remain the baby forever and it all just seemed very unnecessary to me, to be honest. When I finally had this little blonde baby in my arms, I immediately fell in love with her and I took her in as my own. Two years later and soon followed my little brother Brandon. All three of us have had a rocky relationship with our mum so I really did take on that maternal role from a young age.

I couldn't live without Andrea. She is my right hand, my go-to and my calmer when I'm thinking some irrational shit. I don't laugh with anybody the way I laugh with her and, I swear, if I could arrange for a camera crew to follow us around all day every day, we'd be winning a BAFTA. We are so similar yet completely different: I like the limelight, whereas she likes to stay behind the cameras; she was the first to go to university in the family while I didn't make it through two months of college; she's a blonde and I'm a brunette; she has been in a serious relationship for a few years and I belong to the streets – no I'm kidding, I've changed.

We have always been inseparable and we just know we can rely on each other for anything. I have so many memories with her, with the earliest being when I lived at my mum's and I was arguing with her (again) so I decided to run away. My five-year-old sister, being the hype man that she is, wanted to come with me. I still remember walking around with her in London Bridge thinking we were some big women. More recently, I was going through a rough time and I sat on her bed crying, dissecting the whole situation for her. I looked at her and asked her for the answers because she normally comes with some level-headed shit but I think she was fed up with me by this point because she just sighed and said 'Bitch, I don't know. I'm nineteen.'

✧

My brother and I have an interesting relationship. He has acute ADHD (attention deficit hyperactivity disorder) which means he doesn't really like conversing much unless he is talking about things he loves such as history, trading and crypto currency. He is smart as fuck. He enjoys his own company more than ours, especially when he's playing his computer games or building desktops. Recently we've built a closer relationship as we've discovered a common interest in investing. He's so passionate about it and teaches me things that he has learned and tells me where I should invest my money. I'm so impressed by the information he has absorbed! Despite sometimes feeling like we have limited communication, he knows I love him very much and vice versa. I remember once when he was a baby, I had to change his nappy and so I put my pack of Maltesers down to get straight into it. After he was changed, I noticed a Malteser had rolled out the pack so I grabbed it and dashed it in my mouth. I instantly started gagging because, instead of a Malteser, it was one of Brandon's little poo balls that had fallen out the nappy. My mum will never let me live that story down, fucking disgusting.

✧

I really do owe a lot to my Tia Mia and Uncle Niall. These two are basically my parents and they are also the glue of the family. I lived with them from when I was born up until I was eleven and they loved me as if I was their own. I do not know where I would be without them and their guidance. Their love inspires me so much and I am grateful to have them in my life. Everything I work for is for them and my daughter; I cannot wait to be in a position where I am able to buy them the dream bungalow that they deserve. These two taught me the importance of family, the importance of love and the importance of working hard and they have always been the most hardworking people I know. I remember, as a child, cleaning offices with my aunt and I used to love mopping the bathrooms because of the echo when I sang in them. She would always tell me how amazing I sounded and that, one day, I was going to be on *The X Factor*. Success isn't success to my aunt until I appear on that show, no matter how many billboards or sold out shows I have.

My Tia Gloria and Tio Hector also had a huge impact on my life. My mum and I lived with them for a time and I remember, while my mum would be out working, I used to drive my Tia Gloria crazy by constantly begging her to let me wear my mum's dresses and heels, pretending to be in *Dirty Dancing* and *Grease*. They have a daughter who we all call GG and she's practically my younger sister; our favourite pastime now is to go through all of the videos and pictures we have together from when we were kids and just reminisce about all the fun times we had. When it comes to support and just being listened to, GG and her parents have always been there, which my siblings and I will always be grateful for. My Tío Hector is the family dentist (I use the term 'dentist' very loosely). Any time we had a wobbly tooth and it was ready to come out, he'd attach the tooth to the door with floss and, before we could even start crying, our tooth would already be in his hand. When Cataleya's first tooth was ready to come out, I went straight to her Abuelito (Grandad) Hector! It was beautiful to watch what he used to do with me, my siblings and cousins with my daughter; I couldn't help but get teary-eyed because it's these traditions and little moments that mean the most to me. When I envision myself getting married, I've always said I'd start walking down the aisle with my Uncle Hector, who will hand me over halfway to my Uncle Niall, leading me to the luckiest man on this earth, even if I do say so myself. These two men have been the most consistent men in my life and great role models.

> When I envision myself getting married, I've always said I'd start walking down the aisle with my Uncle Hector, who will hand me over halfway to my Uncle Niall, leading me to the luckiest man on this earth.

Overall, I feel extremely blessed to have all of these amazing individuals in my life. I feel lucky to know that my daughter has multiple people who she considers to be grandparents, aunties and uncles and that so many have taken us in, as if we are their own. Being surrounded by love and family is a huge deal to me and it is something I will always emphasise to Cataleya as important. Much like with love, family isn't ever perfect and that is OK, I will just settle for us being perfectly imperfect. Besides, it's kind of fun how chaotic we are.

✧

A Woman Who Inspires
Milena

The most inspirational woman in my life landed in England in the eighties without being able to speak a word of English. As I sit and listen to her tell me her story, I am filled with emotions, from happiness to sadness; I never realised how much my Aunty Mia had actually been through.

Sometimes, I think we forget our parents and older family members have lived too and we never feel the need to ask them questions. But all I want to do now is sit down with a cuppa and listen to everything about Aunty Mia's life so far. I've always admired Mia, she is somebody who has always been extremely welcoming, knowledgeable and pure. Anybody that has met my aunt will tell you about the love that she exudes. She always taught me the importance of family, working hard and being happy no matter what. Now looking back at her life, I wonder how she didn't give up and stayed so strong, but she did and she is consistently motivating me to do better. A beautiful soul, the older Mia gets, the more and more I strive to take care of her, though I know she will never fully allow me to do that. Any time I mention my dream of being able to pay her monthly wages

> We forget our parents and older family members have lived too and we never feel the need to ask them questions.

for her so she doesn't have to worry about her cleaning jobs, my aunt is quick to remind me that I should be saving and investing because she actually enjoys working. That's part of why I admire her – she has a selfless heart.

From the moment she stepped foot in this country, she has worked her ass off for her family and I've never heard her complain. Out of her siblings, she was the first to migrate to the UK from Colombia and she decided that she would bring my mum along after she had established herself. She took my mum in like she was her own and, when I came along, she became my second mum as well. Mia is inspirational to me because, no matter what she was faced with, she pushed on – nothing stopped her. So, when I see her in her large garden at the back of her gorgeous house, surrounded by all of her beautiful blossoming flowers that she adores, I just look at her and think, wow, you actually did it. Those nights that you felt alone and scared, especially when you were a pregnant single mother, you never let it get you down – you always let it motivate you and push you forward.

I remember coming to her when I was nineteen after she had been away in Colombia for a month. Every time she left, I would cry my eyes out because I was so used to being with her and speaking to her all the time, so I made sure I was at her house, ready for when she arrived back in the UK. I'd had an abortion that month and I was feeling extremely low – there was major guilt surrounding my decision. Mia noticed I wasn't myself and asked me what was wrong. I burst into tears and told her everything. I was scared but she comforted me and she told me, 'Mi Hazel, there are lessons in life I can't teach you but I can advise you. Take care of yourself and don't put yourself in these situations in the future, please.' She proceeded to tell me that there was no point crying and, instead, I should figure out a way to ensure it wouldn't happen again. Her loving, yet practical way of thinking always soothed me and I knew, no matter what, that I could count on her. There were times she felt like the advice that I needed was from a man, so she would always say to my Uncle, 'Come on Niall, go and give Hazel some fatherly love and guidance.' I'm always so thankful that she recognised that.

Watching her with Cataleya fills my heart so much that I could cry; I feel like I'm watching myself and, lowkey, I think she feels the same. I am so grateful to God that I've been blessed with that time. I promise to work hard for that woman, she is my everything and, for somebody that wants nothing but love, I cannot wait to shower her with everything she has earned and more. My Aunty Mia, the most inspirational woman in my life.

✧

Tolly

I never knew I was Black until I moved to England. I'd had the privilege of growing up in Nigeria, where my only identifier was being Yoruba. My Blackness didn't separate me from anyone else – we were all Black. I wish I got to hold on to that for longer, to hold on to the years when I didn't have to think about the implications of my race. I was young, carefree and living one of the purest forms of Blackness – Black girl joy. We wore our hair without judgement or care, we laughed loudly and we made up dance routines in the compound. We were unaware of a world where our skin colour meant people hated us.

Race was never really discussed in my household. We all agreed that racism was real, but outside of being told to work twice as hard and to remember that I was not one of my little white friends, race was hardly ever a conversation. Yet, my mum made sure we knew that, in order to get on in England, you had to keep your head down, not make a fuss and just be grateful to be here. It was hard work that was going to get us far in this country, a sentiment I am sure she didn't know is rooted in the fact that Black bodies have always been used for labour. The notion that we are hard-working is down to us being conditioned to work in any circumstance without complaining. Long before Black excellence started to trend, my mum wanted excellence from us. I am Nigerian; excellence is expected. Weekends included doing extra schoolwork and random tests – she wanted us to have all the tools we needed to navigate being Black in England and education, to her, was the greatest tool.

> Long before Black excellence started to trend, my mum wanted excellence from us.

Before moving to Essex, we lived in East London, a place where my Blackness didn't stand out. Our next-door neighbour was Black, my school was full of Black girls, I went to church with Black people and I spent my weekends at hall parties with other Black people. East London felt like a soft landing in the UK. It wasn't until we moved further down the A13 to Dagenham that we faced the reality of racism. There wasn't a day that went by where our race wasn't considered. We were the only Black family on my close and the people in the area made sure we knew we were not wanted. Parents told their kids to come inside when they spotted them playing with us. We had eggs thrown at us, they split the tyres of my mum's car and someone spray-painted the word 'niggas' on our front door. I could carry on listing moments like this. Moments that saw my Black friends and me have dogs set on us, or had us taking the long route home because the shorter route involved walking past a pub. You know what's worse than a racist? A drunk racist. Maybe it's something in the cheap beer that fuels racism, that makes them spurl hatred with such venom. It has to be alcohol that will make a grown man call a teenage girl, half his size, a 'dirty black monkey'.

As well as alcohol I quickly learned that politics also fuelled white supremacy. The BNP, British National Party, won seats on the Barking & Dagenham Council and, at one point, were the second largest party there. BNP spread the notion that ethnic minorities were taking over the borough and the white majority needed to defend itself by any means necessary. My black skin now made me feel unsafe. Racism was no longer limited to name-calling – I could now actually get physically hurt. It was at this moment that we, as a family, realised that we couldn't afford to just sit back and be quiet. We had to defend

> Even though I was born here, this island consistently tells me I am not wanted and it finds ways to remind me that I do not belong here.

ourselves; we had to fight back. We were constantly in arguments with neighbours. I started fighting anyone and everyone that was racist to me. I have never hated being Black but I remember feeling like life, at this point, would be easier if I wasn't.

It is these memories that burn hot in my mind. These memories mean I struggle with my identity as a Black Brit.

Race

Even though I was born here, this island consistently tells me I am not wanted and it finds ways to remind me that I do not belong here. It tells me in its treatment of people that look like me. It tells me by the way it says 'that's an unusual name' after I introduce myself. It's disheartening, it's hostile and it has stripped me of softness because I have had to harden to get through it.

Yet Black British feels like a label that fits. I find myself defending my 'innit innit girls' identity because this part of me has to be about me, not the people who don't want me here. This part of my identity pays homage to the unique experience of being Black and growing up in the UK. It is a celebration of a culture that has been created way before me, one where my story matters. Where I can wear my Blackness as a badge of honour. Being a Black Brit is knowing that I am not really English, because to be authentically English is to be white. It is knowing that my British identity is strongly connected to African and Caribbean traditions. It is knowing that my Christmas roast dinner is incomplete without a side of jollof rice. It is having a strong sense of home, having lived experiences that only other Black Brits can understand.

✧

Being around Black people has always felt freeing for me. Their friendship feels like home, a feeling I didn't get from my white friends. I could never be my truest version with them. I was embarrassed to have them in my house, in case they pointed out things that made me different. Things like us having a bucket bath instead of a shower or my mum who had an accent and insisted on being greeted properly. My friendship group at school was pretty mixed and we all got on perfectly until we didn't. No one argued and there wasn't a fight, but when we got to Year 10, the group split into the Black girls and the white girls. The only thing I could blame it on was visibility – the Black girls were tired of not being seen.

We were tired of doing things we didn't want to do, tired of having to hang around with the white boys who didn't find us attractive. We were tired of having to explain that we couldn't go chill in the park and drink because we weren't allowed out. You see, if a person never really sees you, they can't have empathy for your unique experience. This is something I still find with white women and, even though I have white women who I consider friends, I find the relationships tricky. White women have a privilege that they lean into because it serves their best interests. It doesn't always feel like they are on my side, like they truly love me, for me. Their love and friendship often feels like they love a version of me, the confident, sassy Black girl version. I am not convinced they love me outside of this trope.

✧

This feeling of not being able to show up as my whole self is also one I have felt in the workplace. I have worked in white spaces that felt suffocating, where it was only at the end of the day, when I walked out of the office, that I felt like I could breathe. These were spaces where white women, who were meant to be part of my team, betrayed me, spaces where a white woman questioned my application for a manager role because how could I, a young Black woman, be taken seriously? They have used tears to derail conversations and get away with not being held accountable. I know I keep mentioning white women, without the mention of white men, but it's because I feel like I should expect allyship from white women, because I am a woman. But history and personal experiences have shown me that white women will pick race over gender, every single time. Also, outside of shouting abuse at me, white men just tend to ignore me – they don't see me or my struggles because they are soaking up all of the advantages of white male privilege.

This is why Black love is important to me – the love of ourselves, the love of our communities and of our romantic partners. I feel like Black love loves all of me. In its essence, Black love feels like a protest and it feels necessary in the world we live in. A world where we have to shout, 'Black Lives Matter'. Black love is a safe place to land. As a Black woman, I need all the safe spaces I can get. I am not one who believes that my dedication to my Blackness needs to be validated by being with a Black king, but I do believe

> As a Black woman, I need all the safe spaces I can get.

in the power of Black love. It makes me feel beautiful and it allows me to be seen.

✧

Talking about race can feel exhausting at times. I am bombarded with news, tweets and Instagram videos that remind me of how unkind the world is to Black people. Such reminders can cause so much pain. I've been Black my whole life, I will be Black my whole life and, unfortunately, I don't think I will ever see the end of racism. I know I can't ignore racial issues, but I am tired. I no longer want the responsibility of representing my entire race. At one point, I considered it my duty – it was my duty as a Black woman to be good, to be excellent, to be almost magical. I needed to make sure I didn't leave a bad taste in white people's mouths, not only for me, but for the Black people coming after me. But I am tired, I am a Black woman who grew up poor – how many -isms can one person cope with?

There is a guilt that comes with being tired: it feels like I am betraying my community. To not talk about an issue looks like I don't care, when, in actual fact, I just can't cope. It's too heavy. It's too much to watch people that look like you get killed. I can't turn off my Blackness, not that I would want to, but there's not a make-up wipe I can use that will allow me to fade into the background and have a life untouched by racism. At times, I don't have the energy to keep the fight going, even though I know I can't afford for the fight to end. And when I feel like this, I have to lean on the joys of being Black. I am determined to show Black people that joy is non-negotiable, it is essential, and it is our right. That, even when the news looks dire, the conversation on social media is making them feel worthless and it feels like they are mourning another Black life, they are allowed to laugh.

We need Black joy. We need to hear the familiar sound of Black people laughing and to feel the freedom that comes with handing out the wickedest whine. As a community, we are often told we are too loud so our unfiltered joy is power. I want Black people to allow themselves to do whatever it is that brings them joy. We have faced too much collective trauma to neglect joy; joy says we have hope, in spite of it all. I want us to feel joy and feel deserving of that joy. I want freedom to explore without any limitations. I want to be a baby girl, one who leans into the power that my very existence defies the odds set against me.

✧

Audrey

I started to redefine what my Blackness meant to me a few years ago when I became 'woke'. I've mentioned that, growing up, I was extremely sheltered. This meant that, for the most part, I had no clue how cruel the world was to Black people. Yes, I knew I was different but the full extent of which I heard about this was through my parents telling me I'd have to work ten times harder. I didn't understand the correlation between having black skin and having to be twice as good as everyone else, but I internalised it and tried to live my life the best way I could.

> Being conscious about race, as a young child, meant that I was always performing.

Being conscious about race, as a young child, meant that I was always performing. This really breaks my heart now because it highlights how Black children have to mature quicker and can't truly enjoy just being children. Though Black parents want their children to just be children, they also have to prepare them for the inevitable. It's only now that I've hit my mid-thirties,

I've made the decision to no longer bend myself for others. I want to access my full humanity but there's still so much to unlearn. I spent so much time performing for white people, I don't actually think I knew who I was unless I was around my nearest and dearest. I didn't even know how exhausted I was until I started to actualise what Blackness meant to me and actually live authentically – even now, it's still a struggle.

It's really hard to draw the line between who I am and what I've conveyed to the world out of fear. As someone who can assess situations really well and pre-empt certain scenarios, code-switching became my bag. Code-switching means to changing your style of speech to better appeal to the audience or group being addressed. The craziest thing is that I thought it was a badge of honour to be able to 'adapt' to any environment and I'd often brag about this. On paper, this is something human beings do every day – who we are at work is not who we are when we're with our friends or who we are when we're with our parents. However, as a Black woman, I think the code-switching is far more extensive than what the average person has to do. There's nothing like coming home from a long day of code-switching and breathing a sigh of relief because you can finally just be yourself.

I think I know myself well enough to know that people-pleasing is genuinely a part of my personality outside of adapting. However, adding race into that mix has become quite a dangerous combination for me because constantly aiming to please, alongside trying to dispel every assumption made about me, is a lot. When you're Black, especially a Black woman, you don't have the luxury of being seen as an individual. Stereotypes and racism tend to speak before you do, so you have to make sure you're better than the last Black person but, simultaneously, represent a high standard future Black people. You have to live with the fact that, once you're in that room, what you do determines whether someone else can get a chance. I don't think we talk about this enough and how much this can weigh on you. I've always been very conscious of how my actions will affect the next Black person that comes into a space and it's exhausting. I've always been so aware of my Blackness and how I'm being perceived and it means you're constantly worried about not living up to a stereotype.

I think race plays itself out most in the workplace because it's where you're forced to integrate. Once you walk through those office doors, it's a different world. Being one of only a few Black people in any environment means you're constantly anxious about how you're being perceived, for example, if you go for lunch with all the other Black colleagues you might feel guilt that you're 'segregating' yourself when no one bats and eye when groups of white people go for lunch – it's beyond insane. Think about all the hundreds of people from different walks of life and backgrounds that come together under an office roof – it's unsurprising that this is where issues can arise.

Up until you're at work, you're often in an echo chamber with people you choose to be around and people who are like you. When you're at work, imposter syndrome – feelings of inadequacy that persist despite evident success – can hit you like a truck. 'Imposters' suffer from chronic self-doubt and a sense of intellectual fraudulence that override any external proof of their competence, alongside a sense of being overly grateful for being in a position they earned. My imposter syndrome has always been through the roof at work. Now, don't get me wrong, there's nothing wrong with being grateful for an opportunity but imposter syndrome can often mean you shrink yourself so you don't draw too much attention and tolerate bullshit you shouldn't have to. It makes you think that someone just handed this to you, not that you had the credentials they were looking for.

Suffering from this syndrome in the workplace meant I took a lot of crap from people and wouldn't dare ask for a promotion or more money. I had one PA job where I worked myself to death trying to make the whole team like me. I'd do things that were out of my remit, going above and beyond for people who were quite junior. Half of me wanted to make myself indispensable and the other half hoped it would pay off eventually. When the time came for pay reviews, I thought this would surely be an easy win but, to my shock, mine was rejected. I was in complete disbelief. However, statistics show that Black people and other ethnicities are paid 23.8% less than their white counterparts in London.* Despite the lesser pay, Black women are often expected to do extra labour, stemming from the 'strong Black woman' stereotype that has been around for hundreds of years. We're really expected to do more, for less money, and we're rarely allowed to rest in our femininity. This is why I try to dispel this myth whenever I have the opportunity. Please stop equating Black women to being strong – we're not monolithic and, for every 'strong' woman amongst us, there's a shy and retiring Black woman like myself.

> Despite the lesser pay, Black women are often expected to do extra labour, stemming from the 'strong Black woman' stereotype.

✧

I can't write about Black womanhood without discussing the erasure of the monoracial Black woman. This has always been a thing but seems to be more prevalent than ever right now – it truly terrifies me. Colourism, which is a by-product of racism, is still playing out in the lives of Black women and we're having to continually watch us being replaced with light-skinned and mixed-race women

---

* 'Ethnicity pay gaps: 2019', Office for National Statistics, 12 October 2020, https://www.ons.gov.uk/employmentandlabourmarket/peoplein work/earningsandworkinghours/articles/ethnicitypaygapsingreatbritain/ 2019.

on all platforms and in most spaces. Now, I'm not here to comment on how people identify because it's not my business nor my place, however, it does become my business when I see women who look like me being erased from our own fucking stories.

The flagrancy of the colourism that has been happening recently is wild. One example involved author and mummy blogger Candice Brathwaite, and Rochelle Humes from The Saturdays. Candice had put in years of work researching maternal death rates of Black women in the UK but instead of her documentary being commissioned, a documentary hosted by Rochelle, a mixed-race woman, is the one that's going to air. The media feels as though someone's proximity to whiteness will mean the content will appeal to a wider audience but I'm not buying it. If something is good, it's good and we definitely don't need a type of representation that is 'palatable' to white people. We need dark-skinned Black representation so that little girls don't grow up feeling invisible – so that they can see a different definition of beauty that fits them and, ultimately, so that colourism doesn't prevail. Everything I do is to ensure little Black girls know that they're seen and that they're important, especially when the world is constantly taking from them and not giving anything back.

✧

In March 2020, the world came to a literal standstill with COVID-19, shaking up so many of our lives. Aside from the pandemic, 2020 also became a defining year for race relations after the deaths of George Floyd, Ahmaud Arbery and Breonna Taylor. The world stood together in unity to fight police brutality. Although these stories were specific to America, everyone felt it. There's something about seeing an unarmed man being slammed to the ground and choked to death that made people realise that this shit is real, and it seemed like everyone was taking a stand and speaking out. Half of me thought, *yes, finally*, while the other part of me felt sad because I knew it was just going to be a moment, one that would eventually die down. Before long, everyone would carry on with their lives and the people affected would be left to deal with the aftermath. That's always my concern when it comes to opening up wounds, especially through the trauma voyeurism of Black women's stories and pain – it takes up so much space that not enough shine is given to our joy as well. Black women are not just here as mules, serving everyone, experiencing colourism and being told that we're not good enough or pretty enough. We also navigate this life smiling, with our own unique non-verbal forms of communication and love that we continue to innovate and create no matter the obstacles we face.

How do you deal with racism? The answer, for me, is that I don't. I'm very aware that this response sounds smothered in privilege and, without the work of the leaders and activists who came before me, I wouldn't even be able to write this book, let alone have this mindset. What I mean by this is that racism is a form of oppression that I'm on the receiving end of, and so for me to have to deal with it, as the victim of it, is nonsensical. Racism is a disease and I am the victim – asking me what I want to do about it is victim-blaming. We're able to see why victim-blaming is wrong in many other scenarios, so I'm going to need that same energy to be applied to racism. The burden should rest on the shoulders of the people who perpetrate racism and who benefit, willingly or unwillingly, from white supremacy and the subjugation of Black people; those people should hold the responsibility and weight of dismantling it. Until everyone wants equality rather than power, there's nothing I can do.

✧

I'm hyper aware of who I am as a person. I know my strengths and weaknesses and I feel as though I'm best placed in this world to spread joy, which is why I love what we do on the podcast. Making people laugh and helping them to forget their problems once a week is why I do it. Revolution is like a car and everyone has a role to play to make the car move. I genuinely feel that being part of a project that allows women, in particular Black women, to just laugh and be free is my calling and my contribution to turning the wheels of revolution. I don't think contributing to the cause always has to look like pain, strife, energy and trauma. Figure out what your strengths are and play that part.

✧

Milena

I have to admit that this chapter was difficult for me to start. It was only quite recently that I began to research and learn more about my identity and heritage. I am fully Colombian and I was raised in an extremely Colombian household – which meant music, food, family and friends coming in and out all the time and pure loudness 24/7. I don't remember having a moment to myself at home ever because there was always something going on. Growing up, I didn't have much Latin representation in the media other than J-Lo and Shakira and there was especially a lack (read: zero) of British-Latinx representation. This was one of the reasons I was motivated to be the first British-Latina to make it in the entertainment industry. I wanted to become the representation I never had. It felt like anytime a Latin person popped up on my TV, they were either a sexualised woman with curves and long, silky hair or an impoverished young Latino man turning to crime and violence in order to get by in the world.

There was never any sort of diversity in the Latin representation that we did have, not just the kind of narratives we were given in TV and movies, but also how we looked. If you were to ask someone what a Latina looks like, nine times out of ten they would probably say Sofia Vergara. I've always found this so strange because when I would look at the Latinx people that surrounded me in my day-to-day life, we would all be of different shades with a plethora of hair textures and features. In my mind, there wasn't one set way you needed to look to be Latinx but, in the eyes of everyone outside of our community, there was. I would never have thought twice about seeing an Afro-Latino but unfortunately, there are many people still to this day who don't know that you can be both Black and Latino simultaneously. There are also so many who can't believe that there are Latinos out here with ginger hair or blue eyes. We are so much more than the boxes society has put us in. Growing up, I didn't really take a moment to realise just how problematic this was because I have always had the privilege of fitting into that stereotypical Latina representation. However, I now know how toxic the media (including Latinx media) can be and there is still so much that needs to be done to undo the perceptions created around the Latinx community.

It felt like anytime a Latin person popped up on my TV, they were either a sexualised woman with curves and long, silky hair or an impoverished young Latino man turning to crime and violence in order to get by in the world.

Back in the day, I would catch myself using the fetishisation of Latina women in situations to benefit me because I had internalised it so much. Though I am patriotic as fuck and naturally, when you meet somebody, you will probably describe your pride of where you are from, there were times where I would turn it up a notch to flirt. I didn't feel like I was superior to anybody else, but I was aware of what I could achieve through doing this. Now looking back with all the knowledge I have acquired since, I realise this was wrong. Being Latina isn't a personality trait and this took me a while to recognise. I don't feel ashamed to admit it because I have learnt and grown so much since then and it was something that I had to quickly rectify in order to not perpetuate the stereotypes. Now, if and when I meet a guy and they get overly excited that I am Colombian, I look at the reasons why. Are they too gassed and say things like 'Can you call me papi?' or have they reacted with a genuine comment like, 'Oh my God, I love Colombian culture, I really want to go there!' There's a difference. I know the first guy's full porn history, whereas, the latter is actually interested in the country and what comes with it. It's a huge turn off when men automatically assume that I'm going to just start talking to them in Spanish or that I'd be turned on by some stereotypical shit they say just because they're 'complimenting me'. Whenever I get these comments, I reply, 'Why do you want me to talk to you in a language you don't understand, dickhead?' I ask them questions that they don't know how to answer because even they do not understand what they are saying is problematic and they quickly realise I'm not the one. There are so many other beautiful qualities that Colombian women encompass – we don't need to feed into these warped stereotypes and expectations.

✧

I love being Colombian so much and I wouldn't change it for the world. That being said, what I would change would be the internalised racism and colourism that takes place within our own communities and in our households. I feel like certain remarks have been normalised and, because of this, the elders don't understand how offensive they can be. Respect is huge in my culture so talking back to elders is like giving them a straight slap, but that's how we start letting racist shit slide and I'm not on it. Over the years, I've plucked up the courage to actually speak out and educate, even to older people in my family, as it is something I refuse to ignore, no matter who the person is. I'll be the first to pull people up on their comments and educate them on why whatever it is they're saying is an issue. More time with the elders, there isn't really any point because they've been conditioned for so long that trying to unlearn certain things at seventy is impossible, but I still do my best to try and I make it crystal clear that I don't want to hear that shit around me. I always say it: the change starts at home.

Though there are certain aspects that infuriate me, there are also so many beautiful things that I adopt in my household from my culture because I don't want my daughter to miss out on even an ounce of it. Cataleya is aware that I am fully Colombian and that her dad is half Jamaican and half English – she knows how lucky she is to be able to come from such diverse backgrounds and be able to embrace multiple cultures. Her dad was raised in a Jamaican household, meaning both cultures are very much imbedded and present when it comes to her upbringing. It was really important to us that Cata visited both countries, which she has and will continue to do so (even though that shit's expensive).

A top priority on mine and her dad's list was that she spoke Spanish, not only because being bilingual is beneficial, but because when she's older I want her to be able to communicate with family members here and when we go back home. Her first words were all in Spanish and she had the cutest little accent but that quickly faded away when I moved out of my mum's house. It was quite difficult to maintain the Spanish speaking when it wasn't a language that her dad knew well, so English dominated our household.

> As parents, we have always made a conscious effort to make her cultures known, seen and heard when at home.

Regardless, we still ensure that we are trying our best to speak to her in Spanish, especially now her dad has learned a lot more – she also takes Spanish classes that have immensely improved her confidence. With her going to a predominantly white school in Hertfordshire, I think, as parents, we have always made a conscious effort to make her cultures known, seen and heard when at home. We want her to be confident in her roots and identity – we don't want her to forget it. Best know that Cataleya is having her quinceañera with her chamberlans and damas – a whole ass Mariachi will turn up. And, of course, if her dad wants to do a sweet sixteenth, then I'm here for that too.

✧

I consider myself extremely lucky to have been able to grow up within a Latinx community that helped me feel more connected to my roots, especially because there aren't that many Latinx people living in the UK. Little old me was living it up at Carnaval del Pueblo (Latin Carnival in South London), going Spanish school, taking part in Latin competitions, listening to Latin music on my iPod and being surrounded by Latinos constantly. No one could try and take my roots away from me. However, when I ended up going to Colombia for the first time, I found myself feeling so disconnected. I was too British for Colombia yet felt so Colombian while living in the UK.

In Colombia, I was nicknamed 'Londres', which translates to 'London' in English. They knew straight away that I wasn't brought up there and it made me self-conscious when speaking Spanish. My Spanish isn't terrible, and I do have a Paisa accent because my parents are from Medellín (please refrain from making any connections to drugs, thanks) but, just like with English, there are words that I forget or get wrong – it made me tremendously aware and almost shy. With that in mind, I can understand Cataleya when she becomes hesitant to speak Spanish at times – it feels like people are hanging on to every word you say and waiting to correct or criticise the way you say it.

✧

Being Latinx means having a complex ancestry and I was always interested to learn more about my background and ethnicity, especially as we don't know any of my mum's biological family. My mum was interested too, and I think this is where my fascination with my ancestors probably stemmed from. She was adopted and unable to really go back and see what her mother, grandmother and great-grandmother looked like and that must feel very disconnecting. Something was telling me that I should try and delve deeper into that and so I did an ancestry DNA test.

I've always felt somewhat confused about my identity because I felt like everyone else could easily label themselves as Black or white and it would be an accurate depiction of their culture and background, however, for me, it wasn't as simple as that. If someone was to ask me 'What ethnicity are you?' I'd always answer, 'I'm Latino'. I am fully aware now that 'Latino' isn't a race but it was what I felt comfortable identifying as because it also incorporated my culture into my identity rather than just my skin colour. I'm not going to sit here and tell you lot the ins and outs of every percentage of my results, but I am going to tell you the most surprising thing I found, which was that I am 50% Indigenous. If it wasn't for the test, I would never have known that I have Indigenous ancestors.

For those of you that don't know, Colombians have a diverse background. You can either be of African descent, Indigenous descent, European descent or you could be a mix because of the history of colonisation. I don't know why I never expected to have such a high percentage, I just thought I would come up with a low amount of many places, including European and African descent like my mum's results. I remember the day that it all actually hit me, it was February 2021. I was at a shoot with other Colombian women, speaking on our experiences, stereotypes, identity and more for a series called Latinas Unboxed. I was talking with a beautiful woman that I had met on the first shoot, Díana Bermudez. Of Indigenous descent and hugely knowledgeable, I loved how she was so sure of herself. I showed her my DNA results and she really broke it all down for me – a really defining moment for me. I remember sitting on the panel and actually coming to tears because I felt like I had unlocked this part of me that I didn't know *existed*. I felt overwhelmed and I kept on asking her anything and everything that came to mind because I just felt like I needed to know it all!

This breakthrough has only made me more passionate about my roots and where I come from. Though there is still so much more for me to learn and understand, I am not afraid to say that sometimes I don't have the answers, but I'll try and search for them now for sure. I am excited by this beautiful self-discovery but I am also aware in terms of being careful to not claim to be part of these communities as I don't want to take away the experiences from the people who have had to live through the hardships. Many people pick and choose when to claim things, often when it benefits them, and I'm not trying to offend anybody so what I say when people ask 'what I am', because I also don't want to deny who I am, is that I am Colombian of mixed heritage.

I am conscious that I benefit from white privilege and I use it to bring awareness to issues; I talk on things I know that need to be spoken on and I educate others where I can. It's important to say that these conversations are only just beginning to happen within my community because, for so long, we were just content to say we are Latinos and that is it but it is a journey. When people say knowledge is power, they're not wrong. For the longest time, I was OK with people telling me what they thought I am, or what I should identify as because of my skin colour. I never corrected or mentioned anything because I felt like I didn't have enough education on my roots but now I feel more confident in explaining how I want to be identified.

Spitting in a tube for a DNA lab isn't the only way to find out interesting information about your bloodline though – have conversations with your parents, grandparents, ask questions, research, teach yourself about where you're from. I promise you, you will surprise yourself. There is such a huge strength that comes with knowing what runs through your veins and your identity.

A Woman Who Inspires Tolly

JUNE SARPONG

I've never bought into the notion of never meeting your idols. I not only want to meet them, but I also crave to be respected by them. I have played out scenes in my head about how the interactions would go. Drake would fumble a double kiss and call me fancy – a scene that actually happened. Victoria Beckham would be a little dismissive but would compliment my outfit. And with June Sarpong it was going to be a beautiful moment where I got to hand her her flowers. I would get to thank her for taking up space and inspiring me to do the same. But the day of our meet caught me unprepared.

I was sitting in BBC reception area and I looked up just in time to see her walking out of the building. With very little thought, I followed her. I shouted her name and when she responded I ran towards her and basically spat words at her. I am sure the words made very little sense and, in that moment, my rehearsed conversations decided not to show up. I just wanted her to know that I loved her and I was so grateful to her. If I didn't get to see her on television, I don't know if I would be doing what I am doing. I held on so tightly to the fact that like me, June was a Black woman, not only that but an African Black woman and more importantly she was from Forest Gate, East London, just like me.

A Woman Who Inspires Tolly

And then years later, after that clumsy first meet, I was sat across from her on a Zoom call, interviewing her for my book. Teenage me was freaking out but the me in that moment was proud and grateful, grateful that aunty June was making space for me. We mirrored each other, both sat there holding our cups of tea. I told her that being able to drink your tea before it gets cold is one of my self-care tips. She liked the tip, we cheersed, and I tried to quiet the screams in my head shouting, 'Aunty June, you know!'

Many conversations with people from African backgrounds who have chosen a creative career will include mention of their parents. Our parents have certain expectations of us, they have career paths they would like us to follow, and the media is rarely included in that. Most of our parents are initially against anything that is not academic, and June's parents fitted into this.

'My parents expected us to succeed and if we didn't, there was a problem. The idea of being valued for just being born is not something that immigrant children know. Love is shown when you get an A and disappointment is shown when you deliver a D. So there's no bless you for trying. I don't feel the need to prove myself to wider society, but I feel the need to prove myself internally because of the conditioning I had from my background.'

'My parents were furious when I finished my A levels and decided to work at KISS FM full time, instead of going to university. I remember when I told them, they held a meet-

247

ing. I had aunts and uncles and people I didn't really know telling me I was bringing shame on the family. My dad is the only one who stood by me. He said he was going to give me a year to do this nonsense. I was brought up with my cousins and both of them were going to university so I was constantly compared to them, but it worked out for me in the end. And it's funny because when it did work out, my mother took all the credit for it and told people that she encouraged me to follow my dreams.'

Me and many girls like me are so thankful that June followed those dreams. Watching June on television allowed us to see ourselves and I wondered if she had that. I wanted to know who her June was, who was the woman that inspired her? 'It was different for me; I was a lot younger when I started.' June's first media gig was at KISS FM when she was sixteen.

'I didn't have young Black women on TV as role models. I looked up to Floella Benjamin obviously and Oprah. And on radio, the me for me was Lisa I'Anson. She is a Ghanaian girl also and now a good friend. Lisa was at KISS FM and then left to work at MTV, so my career mirrored hers. Her career was what I wanted, she was riding high on radio, the first Black woman to have a show on BBC Radio 1 and also one of the first Black women to have a mainstream TV show. She was super cool, gorgeous and just like, the hippest thing. And she took me under her wing, like her little sister. So it was so lovely to know someone who had the career I wanted.' Having Lisa go from someone June looked up to, to then become a friend was interesting to me, it reflected a sisterhood that many Black women in the media industry form.

'Maybe I'm wrong, but I don't think that crab in the barrel thing applies to Black women.' June replied after I asked her if other Black women have always been kind to her. 'I really don't. We know how hard it is, we know what we have to put up with. So the idea of impeding another black woman's success is alien to us. I think Black women play a role in society, that because we are women, and because we are Black, we really do understand discrimination from all sides. And we understand how pervasive it can be. And so I think, we have a certain level of caretaking. We are like the mothers of society, we really see where society is going wrong, because we are at the intersection of it and we experience it. Because of that I never had any Black women trying to prevent me from succeeding. I have Black women that supported me, and I always tried to do that for other people.' She continued to fondly talk about the Black women she came up with in the industry. 'There weren't many Black women, but Lisa gave me and Margherita Taylor, who I came up with, great advice. When something big came up we went to her, because she had done it. And then I got to know many other Black women, not just in my industry, women like Valerie Amos, Patricia Scotland, all great women who have been very supportive of me.'

Being around Black women who not only supported me but corrected and showed up for me is testament to who I am today. I make sure that whenever I am around them, I seek advice, I bring up things I am struggling with, I tell them my fears and often their words comfort me or spring me into action. So I asked June how I should balance my work and life. How someone like me, who craves it all, does it all? How do I align my need for a successful career with my need for a family of my own? In that moment June made eye contact with me and said, 'If you do want to have children biologically you must prioritise it, because I think that's one of the lies that we have told a generation. One of the disservices that feminism does for women is that it doesn't always take into account the difference between men and women. The biological clock is real. It's not as early as we have been told or been made to believe, we see women having kids way into their forties but it's more likely to happen for you if you are younger, like your age. So if you know you want to have kids, say to yourself within the next five years I want to have met my person and start my family. And in the same way you know how to prioritise your work and everything that you do, start prioritising meeting the right person. And if there are any internal blocks within you that could explain why you're not attracting the right mate, you have to look into it. It's not just about being with someone, it's about finding someone you actually want to build a life with. And internal work has to happen in order to attract that person into your life. So start now.'

That was just one of the many moments during our Zoom call where June spoke to me with so much love, like she was my actual aunty rather than just someone I watched on television. She shared so much with me, I felt privileged to hear about her experiences, her lessons, her regrets. 'I wish I took the time to really enjoy the moments more because sometimes you're doing something pretty amazing and extraordinary. Like I had so much fun, but I was always planning for the next thing as opposed to sitting in the moment. The best bits are things I look back at. The best first bit was my work experience at KISS FM. I was so young and I was able to see examples of success outside of the environment that I grew up in. Success in people who looked like me and came from similar backgrounds. The great thing about KISS was that it was very multicultural, and it had people from all different walks of life and no hierarchy in the way you usually get. They were loads of people who were kids of lords and all that of course, but they weren't necessarily the bosses. And that's rare, I have never been anywhere else where that's the case. That's why I am so passionate about social mobility because KISS had a work experience programme where they went to find kids like me, we didn't have to go to them. So that changed my life. Getting the gig with MTV, that set me on the path of television and then *T4*. I had so many great moments with that, I got to host Nelson Mandela's birthday party. And then I left *T4* and moved to America. Part of the reason I moved to America was because I had done all that I could do here in the UK. And also at the time I was twenty-nine getting to thirty and youth TV is for the youth and I was no longer a youth, I was a sister and now I am an aunty.

I love being aunty. But I was the older sister then. The writing was on the wall in terms of the options I had, so I moved to America and set up a women's conference, which did very well over there, but I didn't get any TV work from the UK for five years I think. Luckily, I was getting work in the States, but TV execs weren't calling me up in the way they were for my white counterparts in America and there were lots of British people in America. I changed income levels, I had been making a lot of money at a young age, and luckily I am not a big spender but I was also quite cavalier because work was so forthcoming I thought it would always be like that. I thought I would always be able to make that money again. And for a period thank goodness I had savings, because money was much tighter than I had ever had in my life. Not getting work made me rethink how I valued myself and how I was valued by others. I had to make a decision to not allow that to define me. So those were tough times but they were character building.'

The notion of value and confidence came up often during our conversation. Being Black and visible can be challenging and June's experience of it, feels familiar. 'I am very grateful for coming from a community of empowered women, West African women. I was raised around women who thought they were beautiful; you couldn't tell my mum nothing. And you couldn't tell my aunties nothing and whatever size they were they thought they were fierce. I think it was important for me to see that early on so when I went into a world that tried to question my existence I was like nah, if you knew the woman I knew you wouldn't be coming with this. As Black women, we are dealing with colourism and institutionalised racism, so you have to constantly remind yourself of your value and it is work. The media is telling you the opposite of your real worth, so you have to constantly counter that. Ultimately how you feel about you is the most important thing, but if everything outside of you is telling you you shouldn't feel good about you, it's work to make sure you feel good about you. As I have gotten older I have become more comfortable with me and being in the flow of my life. So before I was like, I want to do this by a certain time when actually sometimes your life is telling you something else. I wanted to be someone who controlled my destiny and who wasn't waiting for people to give me jobs or for people to see me. And so I made sure I did other things and knew people outside of my industry and that's what led to this path. I promise you, it works out in the end.'

June for me sits in the space of Black women who have been there and done that, the women who have worked out life and I love being in the company of these women. They talk with such wisdom. I asked June what it was like to be at that stage, and she gave me a gentle look that I have received from many Black women and said: 'You have to know what stage you're in, I am at the stage where I don't work after six unless it's really needed and I don't work on my weekends. I believe in God, I meditate and I pray. But you're in the grafting stage. So when opportunities come, you take them. Don't let your ego get in the way. Knowing where you are in the journey lets you know what you say yes and what you say no to.'

I couldn't let June go without asking her if we would ever get a lip gloss line. 'No, I don't think so.'

Tolly

I don't want to tell you about the years I felt unpretty, nor do I want to focus on the work I did to make sure I knew that, even when the world's version of beauty changed, my own version still endured. I am done with focusing on how the media made beauty feel exclusive to white women or how it devalued Black women's bodies; how it told the world that features which steered far from fair skin, blue eyes and straight blonde hair were unattractive.

> It's time for me to pay homage – homage to all the people who cemented my beauty.

Rather, I think it's time for me to pay homage – homage to all the people who cemented my beauty. To thank the people who fought for me to sit in the affirmation that I am beautiful because to believe otherwise would let them down. And I will be damned if I disappoint the Black women who, with their afro hair, darker skin and fuller figures, shouted Black is Beautiful until it became a movement. What a shame it would be to let down Kwame Brathwaite, the photographer who celebrated

Black identity and, in all of his work, aimed to show us that there is pride in being Black. Even when I look closer to home, how dare I question my beauty when so many of my features mirror the features of the Black women who raised and loved me. To think I am anything but beautiful is disappointing the women who braided my hair, oiled my scalp and invested time to make sure I looked and felt good.

✧

Growing up in Nigeria meant I was never brought up on hating my hair – in fact, I loved it. Doing my hair and spending money on my hair has never felt like a burden to me. Any issues surrounding my hair lives outside of me – I don't see its need to be politicised. I find joy and take pride in it. Its fabric means that I can experiment with it, I have options and I am capable of changing it, whenever I want. My school in Nigeria had us changing our hairstyles weekly, a tradition my mum tried to keep up with when we got to London. I remember having my head nestled between her legs while she braided patterns into my hair. My sister and cousins would cry when it was their turn to have their hair braided but I looked forward to it, I would sit still the whole time and ask to go to the toilet to take a sneak look at the progress. Once I returned home from school on the Monday after debuting my new style, my mum would ask, 'Did you friends like your hair?' It was a question she asked every single time, one my sister and I still ask each other in jest.

My mum is my original beauty queen – she has always believed in looking good. I would sit in her room and watch her apply her make-up. Way before contouring and highlighting, she would powder her face with Fashion Fair, swipe blush along her cheeks, line her lips and apply gold-coloured lipstick. Sometimes, as a little treat, she would kiss me on my lips so the lipstick could leave a stain. All her jewellery would be laid out and she would ask me to pick the necklace she should wear. Once I'd picked my favourite, she would sit on the edge of the bed and wait for me to clasp the hook. In these moments, I fell in love with make-up and dressing up; knowing that I had to wait to be old enough to wear it made it even more enticing. I would secretly experiment with the glitter and frosty pink lipsticks that came free with magazines, neither of which had any business being on my skin tone. I would apply Vaseline on my lips and lids and eventually, I upgraded to clear mascara and hair shop lip gloss once I started getting pocket money.

My prom night was the first time I was allowed to wear make-up. The only time before was when I stupidly cut slits into my brows, a pact that my 'gang', Buff R-Us, and I had made. While I waited for the hair to grow back, my mum would draw in my brows every morning. The gentleness with which she stroked fake hairs into the gaps of my brows was the same gentleness she used to apply my prom make-up. She powered my face with Fashion Fair, swiped blush along my cheeks, lined my lips and, just as she was about to reach for her gold lipstick, I refused and applied my clear gloss instead.

✧

My teenage years saw me looking to other women for beauty inspiration. Although my mum's looks were the staple for me, I wanted to create my own version of beauty and Sky TV made this possible. Sky TV was a Christmas present from my mum to my sisters and me and it opened up my world. I could sit in my living room and, with just a click of a button, I could be transported into another world I didn't know existed. Trouble TV and MTV Base introduced me to so many beautiful Black women – it felt like the golden era of Black beauty on television. These women influenced me so much. It was seeing Spirit's hair on *One on One* that inspired my signature look of pick and drop. What I loved most about these women was that they weren't all the same. They showed so many different variations of what Black beauty looked like. The image of Nia Long appearing on *The Fresh Prince of Bel Air* with her pixie hair is a constant reference for me when I think of beauty. It's a look I still long to achieve. Nia's beauty had me searching for her in movies. Her image sits alongside the image of Tatyana Ali and all the video vixens MTV showed me.

> Trouble TV and MTV Base introduced me to so many beautiful Black women.

260

Long before I knew anything about the misogyny that could be linked with rappers and what it might mean to have Black women on screen being overly sexualised, I was obsessed with the image of video vixens. Seeing Melyssa Ford in Mystikal's 'Shake Ya Ass' video and Bria Myles in Rhymefest feat. Kanye West's 'Brand New' video introduced me to sexiness. Although these videos were not made for my gaze, I was, and still am, fascinated by how these women wore sexy; it seemed to cling on to them naturally and effortlessly. For me, these women are the blueprint for the 'Insta baddies' we see today. Beauty for me does not exist without the mention of hip hop. The vixens and female artists in hip hop created beauty trends without even trying. The likes of Lil' Kim, Aaliyah, Missy Elliot and Brandy further cemented for me that Black women were not only beautiful, but also cool. With very little money, I started finding ways to replicate their looks, buying fake gold hoops, £1 gloss and every hair gel that promised to slick my hair and leave it flake-free (they all failed on that promise). I would even travel from Dagenham to Peckham so I could pay £10 for a full set of nails which matched the nails of these women.

✧

Outside of the physical I also see beauty in confidence. The Black women before me have always displayed an air of 'I look good and I know it.' I remember watching *All of Us* on television and every time LisaRaye's character got a compliment, she would reply with, 'I know.' The act of complimenting plays a huge role in my perception of beauty. There is nothing like Black women complimenting each other. I have found myself going out of my way to compliment another Black woman – it's almost a rule in the Black friend's contract that we stay gassing each other. To believe I am not beautiful would be saying these women are lying. This need to cement each other's beauty is most apparent on Instagram. Under every picture of a Black woman are celebratory cries of 'YASSS' and 'give it to us'. These comments prove that Black women are worthy of admiration and praise.

The way I use Instagram is also worth crediting when it comes to my perspective of beauty. It is flooded with pages dedicated to black beauty. It allows a level of visibility that I never experienced in beauty magazines, both reading them and working on them. It shows women with 4c hair, women who know how to slay a frontal and women who are dedicated to showing make-up swatches on dark skin tones. It's full of tips and tricks that Black women share with each other.

I have always had a special approach to beauty – it comes with pride and care for me. It is how I present myself to the world but also how I show care for myself. Yes, lotioning my whole body every day is to feel the moisturising qualities, but also, it's a personal act of love for my skin and the first act of self-love I was taught – it's almost healing. The ritual of making sure the lotion touches every part of my body, getting a chance to feel my skin and rub past every curve, is one of the ways I tell my body that I love her. This ritualism also shows up when it comes to looking after my hair. Wash days really allow me to indulge. It also allows for a carefree champion pour at the end of my bucket bath. I wash, condition, detangle and moisturise before

> The ritual of making sure the lotion touches every part of my body, getting a chance to feel my skin and rub past every curve, is one of the ways I tell my body that I love her.

deciding what style I want to do. All these rituals were taught to me, nuggets of knowledge passed down from Black women, who used beauty as self-care.

✧

When it comes to paying homage, Black beauticians and stylists deserve so much praise and my relationships with them run so deeply, I fondly refer to them as aunties. So, to the aunties who had makeshift salons at home and the women standing outside shops asking if I want my hair done, thank you. I have categorised these aunties in my head – I reserve cornrows and braids for the African aunties and weaves for aunties from the Caribbean.

Even though I have many frustrations with Black salons, I also have a desire to spend time in them. Black hair salons are not just about hair, they are safe spaces. Safe spaces that are so familiar, even in the design. Most of them house sink basins at the back, a row of seats at the front, with a side table topped with dated magazines. At their best, Black salons are a home for all the variations of Black womanhood to congregate. Every corner is hosting its own conversation and, at one point, stylists will argue about the use of a tail comb. Women with no intention to do their hair will come in and out just for the conversations. And, if you happen to be there on a school day, the kids of the stylists will start coming in after 3 p.m., requesting money to buy treats from the corner shop.

A memory that I hold dearly is being at the salon on the day that Prince William and Kate Middleton got married. The commentary from the aunties was more entertaining than anything on television. They spoke fondly of Diana, wishing she could have been there to watch William get married. They commented on how good Harry looked, alongside cussing William's receding hairline. Being there with them in Upton Park, worlds away from William and Kate, was almost freeing. It allowed a space to laugh and express ourselves without restraint.

✧

I am so lucky to see the beauty of Black women, whether it is legendary women like actress Cicely Tyson, who was the first Black woman to wear cornrows on television, or women like Patricia Bright and Jennie Jenkins, who were the first Black beauty YouTubers I watched and was influenced by. These women, and many like them, have beauty and talent that is timeless, and even if I was not directly influenced by their looks, I am inspired by how they indulge in beauty.

Thank you to the beauty brands who see me, thank you to the YouTubers who create content, the ones who take the pictures I show my hair stylists. And all the love to the Black make-up artists who learned how to cater to Black skin tones, whose handiwork leaves me feeling top tier every time.

✧

cAudrey

I recognised very early on that you got treated differently the better looking you were and growing up, outside of my mum, Blackness wasn't presented to me as a standard of beauty. This is really difficult to write because it makes me realise how much I've had to unlearn, but I promised myself I'd be nothing but honest in this book.

I'd go as far as saying that I was obsessed with white beauty, simply because it's all I saw. It was everywhere: when I watched TV, when I went to school and when I looked at all my friends. I think that when you grow up in predominantly white areas, this is heightened drastically. Outside of my direct family, everyone around me was white and I was othered very early on in life. I clearly remember my reception teacher, Miss Hammond, who I thought was so beautiful, not just physically, but her aura and demeanor, I was four years old, and, of course, she was white. I would put towels on my head and fantasise about having long flowing hair like Miss Hammond. When you're that age, you don't understand the politics of race behind your thoughts and ideas, but this is what exists

266

underneath it all and it shaped my perception of beauty for a long time.

As a child, I was always made to feel beautiful by my parents and family members. They would always affirm me and boy, did I play into it. I was shy but vivacious at the same time and I realise looking back that this validation was so important. However, no matter how loving my family were, it's impossible to block out all the outside influences.

Primary school was the place that highlighted how different I was. At the age of six or seven, I approached the dinner lady, Miss Lee, who would routinely braid everyone's hair in two braids, and innocently waited in line for her to do my hair. When it got to my turn, she looked at me and said, 'Oh darling, I can't do your kind of hair.' I genuinely didn't understand why, then it occurred to me that my hair was in in do-do plaits, a traditional Black girl hairstyle where your hair is parted into four braids and locked in with black thread. My mum would usually add colourful hair bobbles to make it look extra pretty.

I was so innocent I remember thinking in that moment, of course, she can't do my hair, my hair is already done! So I went to the toilet, undid my hair and came back to her. She looked at me and said, 'I still can't do it, darling'. The right thing to do would've been to not to do anyone's hair so that no one felt left out, but this was the early 90s and things were different then – no one was 'woke' or racially sensitive.

When I think of this, I wonder if it could happen now. All I know is that I'd never felt so othered in my whole life and, from that moment on, I knew I was different.

✧

I wanted to dedicate a paragraph here to all the Black girls, women and non-binary people who have experienced colourism. I've written about this in the Race section of this book, but I also want to acknowledge it here, because colourism manifests in beauty constantly. I want you to have something that you can come back to when you're feeling low or being gaslit into thinking it's all in your head.

To all the dark girls who have played second fiddle to their light-skinned and mixed-race friends because they are deemed as prettier or more beautiful in society, I'm here to say the world is messed up and it is *not* on you. As hard as it can be, I promise it gets better. Colourism, or shadeism, really breaks my heart because the world uses Black girls as a punching bag for their internalised self-hate; their ugliness inside is projected on to us and it's not OK. To uplift and celebrate someone purely based on the lightness of their skin is to subjugate someone for their dark skin and it has to stop. I speak to colourism in the Black community

> To uplift and celebrate someone purely based on the lightness of their skin is to subjugate someone for their dark skin.

because that's the community I belong to, but it exists in every country with a non-white majority and is a hangover from colonialism. In Asia and the Middle East, colourism is rife and so I hope this message transcends and helps my non-Black sisters as well – it is a form of oppression that is felt far and wide.

It's not in your head, the problem is systemic and it's not something you can just 'love yourself' out of. Please never forget that you are beautiful and you are enough. Anyone who can't see that can, frankly, go fuck themselves. Highlight that sentence.

✧

Society doesn't allow beauty to be subjective and that's why I think that the phrase 'beauty is in the eye of the beholder' is rubbish because the world has taught us that beauty has already been decided upon and it looks a very particular way. We're all completely brainwashed by this. I've spoken to guy friends who've expressed they have an interest in someone but wouldn't approach them because their 'boys' would question what they're doing with her.

In my thirty-five years of living, I've seen how much beauty can dictate a woman's life and which rooms she can get into. It's such a valuable currency and many of us buy into it. The reception you get when you dress up highly feminine is entirely different to when you wear standard fits and I played the game. I've always been extremely feminine but sometimes it's hard to reconcile if it's actually who I am or if I've just bought into the feminine beauty standard, shaped through the male gaze. Maybe it's both because the two can exist in tandem. I never felt the need to try to dismantle this notion, which may be problematic to some people, but I've always played whatever game I needed to play (within the confines of my own morality) to get what I want. For example, if I had a job interview for retail, I knew how to present myself. When I worked on reception at the PR company, I knew how to present. It would be nice to live in a world where you can present exactly how you want and just be treated based on merit but sadly, we're not there yet.

> I've seen how much beauty can dictate a woman's life and which rooms she can get into.

In dressing up and presenting in a certain away, I know many of us have felt the benefits pretty privilege. Pretty privilege is the ability to navigate through spaces more smoothly because you look a certain way, mainly if you conform to Eurocentric beauty standards, i.e. slim nose, full lips and slim figure. It's largely dictated by how men view you and, if you're Black, it depends on how palatable you are. It's not just colourism, it's also featurism and texturism, which are forms of discrimination related to your physical features and hair texture respectively.

I knew very early on there was a currency in looking a certain way and this was connected to how you're treated even in all-women spaces where you feel pressure to look perfect or compare yourself to those around you – it's actually crazy. I never really felt pretty past the age of nine years old. I knew I was a cute kid but, when you get to that awkward stage where you're too old to be cute and too young to be pretty, that's when you start to pick yourself apart. I never really looked at myself during that stage as I'd avoid mirrors and pictures. I have no photographic evidence of my existence between the ages of twelve and twenty-one. I chose, instead, to focus on my studies and become the funny friend, which ended up being my way through this time.

✧

There's more to life than fitting into the narrow box of society's standards or to be chosen by men. I started to think about which other elements of life hold beauty and one of them, for me, is hopefully having a daughter one day. There's something so beautiful about the thought of having a legacy in my image – honestly, the idea makes me so happy. I've always said that I can't wait to have a daughter so I can see what it might look like being raised by a parent actively trying to dispel misogynistic and gendered standards. Of course, the world isn't free from either of these but being raised with them while also experiencing them in the outside world was definitely a double whammy – I'd love to know what it would look like if you didn't have it at home.

The idea of motherhood and child rearing is something that I've become so obsessed with lately. I never appreciated the beauty of it as much before because I just assumed it was something every woman could do and that it was a staple in life. You get married and you have a baby, simple, right? But, in growing older and having married friends, you start listening to people's experiences and it makes you realise that it's really not that simple. Pregnancy can involve loss, miscarriages, trauma and pain, so to have a child at the end is truly a miracle. If you also throw in the fact that Black women are four times more likely to die in childbirth because of medical racism, pregnancy and motherhood, now more than ever, are both incredibly special and unbelievably beautiful.[*]

> Pregnancy can involve loss, miscarriages, trauma and pain, so to have a child at the end is truly a miracle.

I've learned that it is a blessing, not a right, but I still don't think I'll ever be OK with not having this experience. I've had to do so much unlearning to disassociate womanhood from motherhood and a huge part of that unlearning was recognising that connecting the two meant I was excluding trans women, non-binary people and cis women who may not be able to have children naturally. I began to

---

[*] Hannah Summers, 'Black women in the UK four times more likely to die in pregnancy or childbirth', *Guardian*, 15 January 2021, https://www.theguardian.com/global-development/2021/jan/15/black-women-in-the-uk-four-times-more-likely-to-die-in-pregnancy-or-childbirth.

really dissect why it is I want this so badly and the answer really isn't that profound – I just think I'll make a really great mum and want that to be a part of my story. Having a better understanding of the privilege that comes with motherhood means I've truly been able to see the beauty in it.

Beauty is not just appearance or desirability; it doesn't just mean your aesthetics. Beauty can be found in life in many different places, in our friendships, in our experiences or in motherhood – it's not just skin deep.

TRIGGER
WARNING:
EATING
DISORDER

Milena

In the humblest way possible, I'm a buff ting, and so are you.

We should all see the beauty within ourselves and embrace it, instead of basing our value on how we fit into society's 'standard' of beauty. Don't compare yourself to what you see on Instagram! I am so glad that I grew up pre-social media because I know that the internet would have completely ruined me and my perception of myself. I don't know how the kids nowadays do it and, if you are in your teen years reading this, please do not place your worth on what you see online because nobody is truly 'perfect'. You will be surprised how many filters, photo edits and video edits are being used across the board. At the end of the day, no amount of likes and shares can heal you on the inside; you need to learn to love who you are

> No amount of likes and shares can heal you on the inside.

within as well as your shell, which will carry you through this life.

✧

When I was a young teen, I didn't feel 'pretty' but I knew I had the personality that many lacked so I held on to that. I always made sure that when I walked into a room that my presence would be felt. This lack of love for myself and my image meant that, from a very young age, I developed an unhealthy relationship with food. I only ever used to eat a handful of things and I totally avoided experimenting with foods – I'd always stick to basic things and this only changed in my late twenties.

I remember the night that changed a lot for me. It was 13 December 2003 and, for some reason, I decided to eat a whole advent calendar; who knew that twenty-five mini chocolates would end up with me having an eating disorder? At the time, I had something called emetophobia – an extreme fear of vomiting, seeing vomit, watching other people vomit or feeling sick. In my case, the thought of feeling sick and vomiting was beyond petrifying, I remember any time I felt remotely unwell, I would grab a candle, light it, get on my knees and pray to God to make it go away. Yes, it sounds extreme but, to me, it wasn't, it was a necessary coping mechanism.

Most people who feel sick would go and drink some ginger tea, take some paracetamol or go have a nap but the feeling completely consumed me and gave me an extreme amount of anxiety. My family would always try to reassure me by saying it would subside, which it always did eventually but the severe anxiety I had until it did was crippling. That winter night, I remember getting up from bed, walking into the corridor, looking at the clock which said 3:15 a.m. and just vomiting everywhere. My aunty and uncle woke up and I was shaking from the fear and, instead of going back to bed, I slept on the floor of their room. I was too scared to be alone. I don't think I slept much that night.

The next day, I was still ill and, for some reason that night, I told myself that I was going to be sick again at the same time as the night before. It sounds mad looking back but it's clear to me now that this irrational thinking has been a huge part of my life for a very long time and is closely linked to my anxiety. That day, I managed to convince myself that if I stopped eating then I wouldn't be sick. And that's when my eating disorder began. I stopped eating meals during the day and only ever really drank tea to feel 'full up'. When it came to dinner time, I'd never exceed more than a couple of mouthfuls. My family didn't suspect a thing for a while, as we didn't always eat together at the table, therefore, they couldn't really pay much attention. My aunty's breakfast bar used to have a little gap that would lead to a drawer and I would scoop every meal into that gap secretly – in the middle of the night, I would go downstairs and sweep it all out so it wouldn't stink up the house.

Milena

Soon enough, I began to lose weight quickly. Eventually, my aunt and uncle noticed the physical change and took me to the doctors. I explained what had been happening and they broke down the importance of eating so my stomach wouldn't shrink. That was the first time I heard the word 'anorexia'. As time went on, I would challenge myself to eat two things a day but I never went past that limit, as I was convinced I'd be sick if I did. However, as more weeks and months passed, that 'two things a day' rule would increase until I got to ten foods. By that point I realised that I wasn't going to be sick if I ate more. By this point, I was tiny, constantly tired and pale. At fourteen, I was able to fit into my three-year-old sister's clothes.

The journey was a long one and when I finally got to a point when my eating became regular again, that fear of being sick slowly faded away, but now, left in its place, were concerns about my weight. I had gained a few pounds and didn't want to 'get fat'. The older I got, the more I became conscious of my image. In my eyes, I was the 'bigger' friend so I tried to find other ways to keep the weight off. When I turned sixteen, I came across an article on bulimia and it made complete sense to me. I went from one end of the spectrum to another. I couldn't help but feel slightly excited that I could eat what I wanted but, by throwing up, I didn't have to feel guilty or worry about potentially putting weight on, so that is exactly what I'd do with at least one, if not more, of my meals. At this point, keeping the weight off was my main focus, which made getting over my fear of being sick easy. Nobody knew what I was doing – not my family nor even my friends. I was so fixated on what was staring back at me in the mirror that I didn't care about my health. Making myself sick lasted about six months and then, in the midst of this mentally and physically dark haze, I met Cataleya's dad. I remember having a therapy session about my fear of being sick and eating disorders and my therapist broke it down to me. She said it stemmed from my abuse and not having control over my body, so vomiting felt like danger to me as I couldn't control it, whereas making myself sick felt safer because I was in control and I knew what was coming next. Mad, innit?

> I was so fixated on what was staring back at me in the mirror that I didn't care about my health.

Getting into a healthy relationship did me a world of good. I was eating properly, I was starting to feel like I was coming into myself, and I was a 'good size' which ultimately made me feel pretty. I used to struggle a lot with comparing myself to other girls and I feel like, even now, at my big age, I find myself doing it at times. However, the difference is that now, I catch myself and tell myself what I love about my body, whereas before, I would find myself researching surgery along with plane tickets to Colombia.

It seemed as if I was never content with how I looked and no matter how many compliments or how much attention

I'd get, deep down, there was always something I wanted to change. Growing up in a Latin household also meant that your body and figure were always up for discussion and it didn't matter how many people were in the room, you'd always have a tia or even your mum saying 'Mami ponga cuidado, no vaya comer mucho!' which means 'Be careful, don't eat too much!' They weren't aware of how this kept me in a dark and damaging mindset. I still hear those comments about my body and weight today, which is hard as Colombian women are known for having banging bodies, even though nine times out of ten, it's surgery.

✧

After I gave birth, I found the advice on how to 'lose the mummy fat as soon as possible' from my fellow family members so exhausting. I had been dealing with my weight for so many years that, in that moment, I just wanted to push it to the back of my mind and simply focus on my child and being a new mum. I actually didn't know the physical changes my body was going to go through until after.

For some reason, I just thought my skin would bounce back like all the celeb mums but, instead, the texture was all jiggly and my stomach lost its elasticity, making me feel so ugly. To be honest, it has taken me a hell of a lot of time to feel comfortable with those changes. So, imagine having to get used to a new body and then dealing with people telling you to wrap yourself in clingfilm if you didn't have a faja (waist trainer) and sending you recipes for a bunch of soups and remedies that would eliminate the excess fat. It was intense.

✧

After going through all of this, I can finally say that your mamacita has got to a good place with her body and beauty, and thankfully, I have aged like fine wine. The one thing I know I won't feel fully satisfied with until it's right is my yo-yo-ing weight. One minute I'm on it: exercising, eating well, drinking all the water, stomach on flat flat, ass on what's that, but then it's like I get too comfortable with the results so then I start eating shit again and *bang*, I'm back at square one. Some say I don't want it enough, and I can see why that statement does hold some weight (no pun intended), but it's so hard to stay motivated. I do try to tell myself, 'Milena, you know what it is like to feel uncomfortable in your body but you've never known what it feels like to be completely comfortable' and that really does rile me up like Wiley but, more often than not, that inspiration is overruled by hunger and bad decisions.

It's important to have realistic expectations of what your body can achieve.

Don't get me wrong, I love myself and my body, but I know I could treat myself better when it comes to my eating habits – so that I can be healthier and happier. I know one day I'll feel and look exactly how

Milena

I've always dreamed of and I'm not too far off. I think it's important to have realistic expectations of what your body can achieve because the last thing you want is to feel disappointed and like you've failed, when in reality, no matter how many bench presses you do hunny, your boobs were never going to stand firm under your neck!

At the end of the day, we all need to remember that beauty is subjective. I do honestly believe that somebody's aura and who they are on the inside can do a lot more than what meets the eye. Some women have this vibe that they exude and I'm just in awe. There's so much pressure on the physical that we often forget that we have to work on our inner selves if we ever want to feel 100% happy. If you're reading that and you don't feel happy with something about yourself, know that you're not alone. But, crucially, no matter how many followers or 'likes' people get, you shouldn't make it your goal or aspiration to look like them. You are you and that is beautiful. There is only one unique version of yourself in this whole world, so why live life hating it?

All the questions you wish you asked the men you dated

You see, these questions are not because we want our exes back or anything, nor is it that we are pinning our view of ourselves on how they view us. These are just things we have always wanted to know – questions left unasked, things left unsaid. So, we're going to amuse ourselves; maybe having it out on paper will mean we can stop thinking about them, move on or help others with the same questions.

Here are just some of the questions we have for the men we've dated, and if any of you are reading this, don't text us.

Tolly

What god do you pray to?

I ask this because I assume you have exclusive access to a god. A god who lets you know that I am doing OK and no longer thinking about you, because every time I got to this point, you would contact me. A 'hey' or 'just checking on you' – the bare minimum, but yet, it lingered and would send me right back to craving you again. So, who is this God, and does he allow new sign ups?

Do you still have those leather boots I left in your house?

This is my own fault. I had left them there as a way to mark my territory, something that showed other women that this was my space. However, it would be great to know that you have not thrown them away, because, you see, those boots are the only real leather thing that I've ever owned. A treat for myself. Honestly, I would do anything to have them back, anything but talking to you, of course.

The Dating Tea

What initially attracted you to me?

My ego is coming into play now. I want to know what it was about me that attracted you – was it the exchange of looks we shared at that party? Me positioning myself so you got the full view of me? What was it that made you think, yeah, I'll have some of that?

What is your favourite memory of us?

We can both agree that, in amongst the bad, were the good times, like really good times. Like the time we exaggerated what we were to the Uber driver. We told him that we were off to secretly get married and he spent the whole journey trying to talk us out of it. What is a memory of us that makes you smile?

Did you notice the exact point when it was over?

Because I saw it in you. Long before we actually called it quits, we both knew it was done. I don't know if it was familiarity that made us stay or if we just didn't want to accept it was over, but did you feel it before I said it out loud?

Could this be a case of the right person, wrong timing?

Would this be different if we were both in different spaces? I know I have the tendency to not follow my heart but, instead, be led by a timeline I have in my head. So if we met at a different time, could it have worked?

When did you feel the most loved by me?

I like to pride myself in how I show love – everyone I love, or feel love for, knows it. It would be good to know the things I did, both big and small, that made you feel loved and made you feel seen.

How many people did you tell I was crazy?

I take accountability. I moved mad, not often, but enough to be deemed 'crazy'. But do you ever think about the role you played in this? What am I saying? Of course you don't.

Did I really have something to worry about with that girl you said I shouldn't worry about?

I don't ask this because I want to torture myself by comparing myself to her. I just want to know so I have evidence to back my statement that women's intuition is very real.

Was the sex bad for you too?

Because, honestly, it was awful for me, and surely our experiences can't be that different considering we shared these moments together.

Audrey

Why did you pursue me so hard then sleep with my friend?

So this question is for my first ever boyfriend who shall remain nameless in print but was the perfect gentleman in his pursuit of me. He's the one that would say, 'Audrey, when you gonna be my girl?' every time I walked past for two years, until I eventually replied 'today'. I then found out that, not only did he cheat on me, he cheated with a friend. What I want to know is why? What was it about her? I feel like this was the start of my distrust of men. I'm over it now of course but I'd still like to know what I did to deserve this treatment.

Why did you only see my value when other men showed interest?

Can anyone else relate? I'd been 'seeing' my ex for months and months and there was never any urgency in making it official until he heard through the grapevine that another guy was interested in me. This guy was planning to make a move if we weren't official and surprise, surprise, I became a girlfriend soon after.

Why did you say the teddy bear belonged to your niece when it belonged to one of your three daughters?

I dated this guy, who I can now admit I was obsessed with, but when I look back, I don't know why. I was at his house and found a child's teddy bear and when I asked him who it belonged to. He looked me dead in the eye and said his niece. Turned out he didn't have a niece but he did have three daughters under the age of six.

Why didn't you try harder?

I was once told by a man that he wanted to fight for me but, at the time, he didn't even know who he was and what he wanted. Because of that, things just fizzled out. At the time, I wondered why he didn't try harder, but, as a grown woman, I now know he just didn't want it enough, if at all.

Were you really sorry?

If I had £1 for every time I've heard 'I'm sorry' with no changed behaviour, I'd be a millionaire. So I'd love to ask the men I dated in the past if they really meant all the apologies, all the it'll never happen agains, all the take me backs and the forgive mes too.

Milena

Were you ever going to leave her for me?

I talk about the time I was a side chick often and I normally laugh it off, but the truth is, this one cut me so deep. I didn't know about her in the beginning – I fell in love and I wanted to believe that the feeling was mutual. A few years in and I was still in the same position, though I did my thing during that time because I'm not a complete dickhead! He was somebody who always got me, no matter what, and I honestly believed him when he said he would leave her for me, but did he mean it?

Did you ever truly love me?

Words are a beautiful thing but when you act in a contrary way to them, it makes a woman question it all. If you loved me, then why weren't you with me? If you loved me, then why weren't you by my side? If you loved me, then why didn't you make me 'the one'? These are the thoughts that hit me mostly at night. I often wonder if it was just infatuation rather than love; if it was lust rather than me being 'the one'. I guess the proof is in the pudding – he's not with me so that's that.

Was the love you had for me based around my success?

I mean, I'm no Ariana Grande, but I am kind of in the public eye (feels weird saying that). This means it's easy to question people's intentions, especially men that you date. I automatically turn off of a guy if he asks, 'Am I going to be another story on your podcast?' Sir. Fuck off. With this guy, I started noticing patterns – any time I was celebrating something, he would pop up from out of the blue, congratulate me and then, all of a sudden, want to see me because he was so 'proud of me'. He would say he 'wished things were different', knowing full well if he really wanted to be with me, he could have done so. This all lead me to believe he just wanted to be a part of the good sides of my career or that he might just be clout-chasing.

Did you ever feel guilty for what you put me through?

How do you sleep at night knowing how you hurt me? I wish I could have climbed into your body and actually felt the things you felt because, maybe that way, I might have understood. I remember sobbing my little butt off in bed over you, knowing full well you were caressing another woman's body without a care in the world. Has it ever dawned on you the pain you caused? I know it wasn't all you, as my toxic tendencies allowed you back in every time, but I still feel my intentions were pure.

Are you proud of the woman I have become?

You watched me grow into the woman I am, you heard about all my hopes, dreams, ideas and ambitions, and though destiny had its own plans for us, I often wonder whether you're proud of the person I've blossomed to be without you. I know you are deep down inside, at least I hope you are.

Do you think I asked too much of you?

Sometimes looking back, I wonder if I asked too much from a couple of people that I was with. I don't mean material things, but emotionally – I know I needed constant reassuring without me realising that the love I wanted so badly was actually from myself. There were moments that I felt unloved and unwanted by the men that I was with and I didn't understand why. It would make me think, is it me?

Did you ever really forgive me?

I made a mistake, a mistake that would cost me many years. Though you eventually told me you had forgiven me, I've always felt like your actions said otherwise. I felt like

I was constantly paying for a stupid decision that I made when I was an emotionally lost nineteen-year-old. Though you've remained in my life, I do wonder if deep down you truly closed that chapter or if there was anything else you would want to talk through so we can really move on.

Did you push me away on purpose?

When you hurt people and they let you back in, they build a wall, a wall that will take a lot of work breaking down. They naturally protect themselves but, within that process, a lot of shit happens. You end up being spiteful, hurting the one who hurt you and pushing them away, even when you know that person has changed. I felt that you didn't really want to make the effort to work past these things, so you pushed me away instead.

Do you wish I left you earlier?

Did you feel like I wasted your time? I hope not, because I feel like the relationship taught me a hell of a lot. It was a transitional period of my life. Things didn't become what we imagined and it took almost two years to get ourselves together but, for me, it was worth it. Looking back, I think had I permanently left the first time we had broken up, neither of us would have learned the important lessons know now. I hope you don't regret the time we spent together, but I'll never know if you do for sure.

Your Dilemmas Solved

Now, this wouldn't be a Receipts book without some dilemmas. And as we expected, our listeners have plenty! So we're bringing problem pages into books now (you saw it here first).

Tolly

How do I get over a break-up and move on with my life?

I was once asked what is the most pain I have felt that was not physical, and outside of grief, my answer is heartbreak. Thankfully, and unlike grief which seems to stick around, while always altering its volume and presence, heartbreak goes away. The pain from a break-up will not always be there. You will be happy again, you will get over this person and though it might feel unrealistic right now, you will love again. Annoyingly, the cliche is true, the passing of time is the only remedy to getting over a break-up. But during this time, you can do things that make you feel good. Of course, this will be after you have thrown yourself into a pit of despair and found the bottom of many ice-cream bowls – Ben and Jerry's Cookie Dough has always been my preference. Take this time to put yourself first, to re-evaluate what it is that you really want, and to spend time with your friends and family. I would even say wear less and go out more. But if you listen to anything I ever have to say, it should be this: let go of the idea of closure. The want for closure is just a hope that you will discover what went wrong so you can undo it and get back together. The search for a narrative that might make sense of what happened keeps you holding on because you're never actually looking for closure, you're looking for answers; answers that might give you an opportunity to change the outcome. And that doesn't help with moving on or feeling better.

I feel lonely and I want to make more friends. How do I go about that?

Remember how easy it was to make friends as a kid? All you had to do was ask. You picked someone, you asked, and just like that, you were friends. Hand in hand, with matching pigtails, you skipped away across the playground. But the older you get the harder making friends becomes. It seems like everyone has their friends already, making little space for new friendships. The key to making friends in adulthood is intention, and it requires effort. It is going out of your comfort zone, finding clubs/groups of people online and in real life who share your interests. It is not just saying, 'We should do drinks', it's actually going for drinks, and then seeing them again after that. As scary as it might feel, you need to be vulnerable. This can be hard because I know the feeling of loneliness can make you more aware of rejection. But to truly dive into making friends you need to let go of that fear of rejection, and you will discover that more people are open to new friendships than you think.

It feels like everyone around me is doing well and I'm not. They've all got exciting jobs and I'm still stuck in a workplace I hate. How do I stop comparing myself and feeling down about this?

For as long as I can remember my mum has repeated this saying in our home: 'Not all fingers are equal.' In this, she means that even on the same hand, on the same body, all five of our fingers have different sizes, shapes and uses. This has always brought me comfort. It reminds me that I have my own use and that my journey is different. Every time I think of that saying it stops me from using other people's journeys and successes to highlight my shortcomings. We live in an announcement culture where social media is full of people's best bits and this means we are often comparing our worst bits to everyone's very best. Rather than focusing on what everyone else is doing, it's important to use that energy on working on yourself and becoming the person you want to be. What is it that you want to do? What does a job you love look like? What makes you excited? What small thing can you do every day that allows you to reach the big goal? Comparing yourself to others will make you feel lost, it deprives you of joy and takes focus away from all your achievements big or small.

I don't feel in touch with my culture, how can I change that?

I feel most in touch with my culture when I am around people who share it with me; people who can speak the

language and people who understand and appreciate all
the nuances that come with culture and heritage. If you can
travel to the country that's great but I think the best way to
get in touch with your culture is to be curious about it. Eat
at restaurants from your culture, read books about it, listen
to podcasts made by people of your culture. Immerse yourself in it all, whenever you can.

Audrey

I'm not unhappy with my partner but it also doesn't feel quite right, and I feel bored. When do you know if it's the right time to leave?

Firstly, I think it's important to interrogate those feelings before making any impulsive decisions. Why do you feel bored? And what have you done recently to make things interesting? Relationships definitely go through quiet moments and it's important to identify if it's a just a more mundane period or if you've fallen out of love with your partner. Try and spice things up if you can and create more intimate time for each other. Go on dates, bring them in on any hobbies you might have or find something you can do together that's new. If you feel like you've exhausted all measures and you're still feeling the same maybe it's time to move on, but it's worth having an open conversation with yourself and your partner first. Ask yourself whether you're still in love because that's very different to loving some-one. Once you've figured that out you'll know what to do. It's OK to break-up with someone because a relationship has run its course or it isn't serving you anymore. Embrace your inner strength and do what feels right.

One of my close friends has changed up on me and is making me feel bad about myself, should I end the friendship? And if so, how?

Toxic friendships are awful because we often set a different standard for our friends than we do partners or acquaintances but that doesn't mean it's acceptable to tolerate anyone crushing your self-esteem. I think it's important to let people know how they're making you feel before ending anything to give them a chance to explain themselves and make a change. This open communication is important for you to get the answers you deserve and it also might save the friendship from falling apart. If you don't get a good enough response or they don't make an effort with you afterwards then you can end the friendship by telling them your boundaries have been crossed, or if you're non-confrontational, start to remove yourself slowly.

How do you navigate a toxic relationship with one (or both) of your parents?

The parent-child relationship is complex because we're socialised to believe it's supposed to look a certain way but this definitely isn't everyone's story. I'm a firm believer in centring yourself and your wellbeing and sometimes that might mean giving people (parents included) limited access to you. I think some grace can be extended in understanding that not everyone can be good parents but most importantly you should not be blaming yourself for their short comings. If you're in a position to seek help, therapy is a great way to talk to an unbiased person about your situation and that will go a long way to help you heal, especially as parent-child relationships are so fundamental to understanding ourselves. Putting boundaries in place with your parents, knowing when to walk away when things get tough and disengaging from conversations that cause pain are all things you can do to help navigate the relationships moving forwards.

I've been offered an incredible job in New York, but my partner's job is in the UK and he doesn't want to leave. I love him so much, but this job is a once in a lifetime thing, what should I do?

Once in a lifetime opportunities don't come around often and I think you owe it to yourself to give it a try. Have you considered long distance? People make it work all the time and I wouldn't end your relationship straight away because you are worried about being apart. I would see how long you can have both your new job and your partner for and take it from there. You don't want to be in a situation where you wonder what if or where you come to resent him for limiting your experiences. If long distance doesn't work out, you could always come back to the UK and pick up where you left off.

Milena

I haven't had sex yet and I feel like I'm the only one. When do you know if it's the right time to lose your virginity?

Don't put unnecessary pressure on yourself. Honestly, you need to remember that everybody's journey with sex is different. There isn't a 'lose your V card' day when you're supposed to do it, it all comes down to when YOU feel ready. And the truth is, in that moment, you will know, but until then don't watch others and don't overwhelm yourself with all of these thoughts. It's normal to be a virgin at any age and you're not less of a person because you haven't had sex. I think it is important especially for women to take ownership of their bodies and their sex lives. Please do not allow anybody to convince you to do it or make you feel bad – trust yourself and know that when it happens it will be good because YOU decided to do it. As well as this, make sure you don't have any expectations for your first time, it's definitely not what the movies portray! Just enjoy it as it comes. Literally.

Milena

I'm not attracted to my partner, what do I do?

I think it's important to have that physical attraction to your partner but I'm wondering what's changed from the moment you met them as I'm sure there must have been something you were drawn to back then? Ultimately, we all deserve to be attracted to the person we are with and if that has gone or faded away then it's probably time to leave. But I would take some time to consider this first, because sometimes attraction can come back and you might just be going through a low period yourself, and it's impacting on how you're seeing your partner. Also don't forget, we are all going to get old and haggard at some point so isn't the love you have and the family you have built more important? Think on it for a while. Ask yourself what means the most to you and if it's a dealbreaker and they repulse you, I'd definitely 'Peace up, A-Town down' and leave them sis.

I hate the job I'm currently in and want to start a career in the creative sector. It would mean a pay cut though, and everyone says it's a hard field to be successful in. Do you think I should take the leap or persist where I am?

I think you should do what will make you happy regardless of the risks or what people say. You hate where you are at the moment and life is too short to be somewhere you despise. Yes, there may be a pay cut but you can't put a price on good mental health and you could potentially work your way up and end up being paid more than what you are on now. Take the jump, it may be scary and it may not be easy but the experience you will have and the lessons you will learn from it will be worth it all!

How do you know you're ready to date casually, and how do you keep that intention in mind so you can just have some fun without the feelings?

You have to be honest with yourself and ask yourself if you are somebody who would enjoy casually dating. Not only that, are you someone who can keep your feelings at bay? If you have asked yourself the important questions and still feel happy to move ahead then please read on, but if you're somebody who falls in lust quickly, gets attached and fantasises about a fling turning into walking down the aisle then I would stop here and accept you're a romantic and it's not for you. The most important thing here is knowing yourself. I don't think there is a specific feeling that indicates you are completely ready, but I do believe that overthinking it and putting pressure on yourself detracts from the human experience and enjoyment of dating. If it feels natural and good, go for it and get that free food!

Acknowledgements

Tolly

There's no way I am going to write my acknowledgments and not start it with Glory Be To God. It would be un-Christian of me, but mainly, it would be un-Nigerian of me. Every Nollywood film I have ever watched ended with the closing line, Glory Be To God. But in all seriousness, it is down to His glory. I am strengthened by my faith in Him, and at times, when I had very little to reach from, I would say a little prayer to feel full again.

This book was written in the time when COVID-19 stopped the world and, although it would seem like the stillness would allow for the perfect time for writing, it didn't. I stared blankly at a laptop screen for days on end with very little inspiration to write. I was riddled with doubt and fear, wondering if I could really do this. I'd think, what if the book is pure shit and it doesn't make a difference to the lives of anyone reading it? Those doubts were quieted by looming deadlines and the realisation that this was just my chance to tell my story thus far. Plus, my stories are great and writing them felt good. So, after God, my next acknowledgment is myself – I did this even when it was hard, I did it, I'm an author.

Acknowledgements

Audrey and Milena, honestly from the bottom of my heart, thank you. My favourite memories now have you both in them. I am so proud of us. This journey – it's not the end as we still have way more epic shit to do – has been so amazing. I cannot believe that we are here. What started in Dan's studio, where we would have to drink to record, is now a bestselling book (this is not a fact, I am just manifesting). We have recorded when we didn't want to, had to show up for each other, cover each other's backs and dealt with the good and the bad of this so gracefully. I am happy I get to share all this with you guys – can you actually believe this is a real thing we are doing? We have reached heights that leave me amazed. I sometimes look back at what we have done to take it all in. We have achieved more than I could ever have imagined. You have both taught me so much and we are now forever linked.

To my family, writing my chapter on you guys brought me so much joy. Mum, thank you. Shout out to you every single time – you are the love of my life, my best bits come from you and my best writing comes when I am writing about you. Damilare, you have always been my biggest fan, your daily phone calls keep me sane. With every race I have ever run, you have stood on the sidelines cheering me on, and when I have felt unable to carry on, you have joined me on the track and run alongside me – thank you! To my brother Femi and my sisters Fumnilola and Jumoke, I am so proud to be your younger sister. Thank you for living your lives in ways which allow me the freedom to be creative. I am most grateful to you guys for my nieces and nephews, I love them so much and vow to always be their cool aunty.

My friends, GANG GANG! You will recognise so much of this book because my stories feature you all. Thank you for being who you are, for being patient with me, even during the times when I become self-absorbed and complain about shit that really doesn't matter. Because of you guys and our group chats ('Influencers & Aisha', 'GANG', 'Girls' Night'), I am balanced. You give me reason to laugh every single day – you are my real friends, the ones who always show up way before I even ask. Tamika, our friendship is my rock, I love you so deeply. You are the leader of the Get Shit Done gang and the way you manoeuvre through the world, soaking up every opportunity, fuels a fire in me. Toni, thank you for being so giving, for knowing what to do every single time. You are a Godsend and there's not a thing I would not do for you. (I am sure you all know that I am typing this while crying, a single tear just dropped on my laptop and it felt filmic.) To Ade, your insults have encouraged me more than you know, your 'get out of bed, you lazy shit' texts contributed to me actually getting this book done. Gena, thank you for reading the random chapters I sent you and allowing me to believe I could actually do this, I can't wait for the world to read your stories. Jacob, my G, thank you. The kindness you've shown me has left an imprint on my very being. Also thank you for your music because, in times of chaos, it calmed me. To Julie, thank you for opening up my world. Your perspective on the world and the questions you ask allow me to dig a little deeper.

Kat, the agents of all agents, I don't know if you saw it panning out like this when you slid into my DMs but I am so thankful you did. You have changed my life; you saw a potential in me that I didn't. You get it, you get me, and that means everything.

To our editor Katie, thank you for your patience and for believing we could actually write a book. I mean look at us, who would have thought it . . . you, you thought it. It feels like so long ago when you and I stood on the rooftop of Hachette's offices talking about what a book from me would look like. I appreciate you so much.

To everyone who has ever listened to *The Receipts Podcast*, you are the best. From the very first episode, you have shown me so much love. You fondly refer to me as your friend, your sister and your aunt and all of these titles are such privileges to hold. You have changed my life.

To all the Black girls and women who have loved me, hired me, rooted for me and messaged me. The ones who see themselves in me and found the space to slot me into their lives. Thank you. I pray you all feel the love and kindness you have shown to me.

Love for the love, my Gs.

Audrey

Funnily enough, this has been the easiest part of the book to write because, without the support of these individuals, I wouldn't have had the knowledge, the stories and the experiences I've been able to draw from for the podcast and this book.

My first acknowledgment has to be the highest of highs – the Lord I serve is a great one and, without the presence of God in my life, nothing would be possible. I'm not going to pretend to be the best Christian on earth, but I know God is working in my life.

To my immediate family, Johnny and Angelina Indome, Vanessa Indome and Jake Indome, thank you for your constant love and support, for being my number one fans and being my safe space at my lowest times. Thank you Mummy and Daddy for being such an excellent example and giving me the best childhood I could ever ask for. Daddy, thank you for being a stand-up man who has shown me what being a good person looks like – your patience and kindness has shown me not to expect anything less and

Acknowledgements

I love you. Thank you Mummy for all you've done and continue to do for me. You always put yourself last and if I can be a fraction of the woman you are, I'll be happy.

My best friend Rachael Cassidy, thank you for the memories, the love, support and the inspiration. Thank you for holding me accountable, always letting me know how great I can be and for always seeing the best in people and situations.

Nicholas Akande, even though we've been on a rollercoaster full of highs and lows, there's no way I could write a book and not thank you for being my rock in the darkest times, for the pride you took in everything I did over the years and the emotional and physical support you gave me, because of the man you are, I was able to shine guilt free.

To Tolly and Milena, you've become like sisters to me and I couldn't imagine doing this journey with anyone else. Through the highs and the lows, you've kept me going, made me laugh till I peed myself a bit but, most importantly, you've changed my life forever and I'll always love you.

To my grandmothers, Teresa Esi Mill and Caroline Indome, thank you for being the women you were so I can be the woman I am. You made sacrifices so I can live the life I live and there are no words to describe my love and admiration for you both, I hope I've made you proud.

Audrey

Renay Richardson, thank you for seeing the vision from the very beginning. I'm so glad the industry is giving you your flowers because you deserve them. Not only have you been a beam of knowledge, you've been a friend. Without your vision, none of this would've been possible.

Katie Packer, thank you for championing us so we were able to get this book deal and thank you for your patience with us when we missed every single deadline! Most importantly, thanks for letting us be authentic and real and just for the opportunity of a lifetime.

Kelechi Okafor, thank you for doing the work so I don't have to. Thank you for sharing your knowledge and breaking it down in a way that's digestible for people like me. Thank you for putting your neck on the line daily – they don't know it now, but they will know. Thank you for being a baby girl.

To my future children, look what Mummy did! Cherish this forever.

Last but not least, thank you to our listeners. I don't actually think you understand what you've done by simply supporting us, I wish I could personally thank every one of you individually for changing my life forever. I love you all and may all your hopes and dreams come true whatever it is you decide to do.

Milena

So, as you can tell I've been through a lot. I don't think I would've been able to overcome all of these situations without God and certain special people in my life. I've always been the 'life of the party' but there would be no party without the following individuals, so I really want to take this moment to thank them.

First and foremost, I want to thank God. For blessing me and for always keeping me going when I felt like giving up. The life I've led hasn't been easy but it has always been covered by him. The good and the bad have all been lessons for where I am now, and I know in my heart I should trust in him more.

The biggest blessing in my life, my daughter Cataleya. I want to thank you for being such an amazing little girl, for brightening up my day without even knowing and for giving me a purpose in this life. Mi hija, everything I do is for you and you have already made me the proudest mama ever. I cannot wait to watch you blossom into the beautiful little person I know you are destined to be.

My sister Andrea, my best friend, my right hand, I adore you. There are not enough thank yous in the world to show you my appreciation. You are the young woman I hope Cata grows up to be like. Never forget how amazing you are and I promise to always do the best I can as a sister/mum for you. I love you more than you know.

I really want to say thank you to my baby father Kyle for putting up with the madness, for always helping me when it comes to my career, for being there and for being the world's greatest papa to our daughter. Thank you for showing Cataleya the definition of a true man. Thank you for never leaving and for always being a phone call away. We appreciate you.

Thank you to Aunty Mia and Uncle Niall for always believing in my dreams, for always pushing me to strive for the best and for taking me in as a child. You both have taught me so much and I am eternally grateful for it all. I love you both with my whole heart and more.

I want to thank my mum for trying her best. I know through it all she loves me and, even though we haven't had the easiest of times, I do love her very much and I am grateful for the fun times we have shared together.

I want to thank Teresa Simone (Madre) for always supporting me, for loving me like her own, for showing me what a strong woman looks like and for always being there to make me laugh. I will never forget our Jamaica trip.

Acknowledgements

Thank you for accepting me into your household the day I came and never left!

I want to thank Colin Batsa for never giving up on me, for believing in me no matter what, for always pushing me, for being the greatest godfather to my daughter and for the support and friendship I've had over the last twelve years. Love you so much Coco, really appreciate you.

Oh gosh! A HUGE thank you to my closest friends, Alice, Shan and Anita. Thank you for always being there for me, for wiping away my tears, for your honesty, for always making me laugh, for being part of some of the best memories of my life, for the love and the constant support. I don't know where I would be without you girls. I am truly blessed. I love you all so, so much!

Thank you to my beautiful cousins Natasha and Jeni for being there for me, regardless of distance. You're my family first and foremost but more like my sisters and I am so, so grateful to have you both in my life. Sanchez bloodline!

A massive thank you to my therapist Yasmin. I know you say I saved my own life for taking the steps to getting therapy and wanting to work on myself but you have contributed a huge part to me being who I am today. Thank you for always reassuring me, for always reminding me to be kind to myself because of all my traumas and my past. I don't know where I would be without you. Through all the tears, laughter, anxiety and confusion, you've been there to settle my storm. Words do not amount to how much our sessions have completed me. All the missing and shattered pieces now make sense because of you, us, and I'm so grateful!

I want to thank the girls, Tolly and Audrey for being on this journey with me, for sharing the same visions, for all of the hard work and for all of the fun times. Wouldn't be the same without you both. The highs and the lows we've pushed through together are amazing and it just shows that this was meant to be. I'm proud of watching you both grow as women. Love you.

Katie, thank you so much for all of your hard work, for helping and guiding me through this book and for always being there to listen to my dumb questions and ideas! Thank you for giving me the confidence that I lacked when I first started writing and for always being reassuring. I truly appreciate you.

I want to thank the person dealing with my shit at the moment. You're amazing. We got this.

The biggest thank you is to the listeners and supporters; you've changed our lives and without you this wouldn't be possible. You mean so much to us and sometimes I almost can't believe how long we have been doing this because of you lot. I will keep thanking you all for the rest of my life!

Resources

We realise that in some of these essays we have written about some deep and potentially triggering things. When we said no filter, we meant it! So, we've decided to provide these resources in case any of the words in this book have brought up unresolved feelings for you, or if you are struggling currently and seeking help.

Never be afraid to speak up. You are important.

MENTAL HEALTH

Mind provides advice and support to empower anyone experiencing a mental health problem. You can access information about different experiences, treatment and support options on their website and Mind's InfoLine is open 9 a.m. to 6 p.m., Monday to Friday.

https://www.mind.org.uk/

0300 123 3393

Resources

Samaritans will provide emotional support to anyone who is struggling, with specially trained volunteers available to listen by phone or over email, twenty-four hours a day, seven days a week.

www.samaritans.org

116 123

We know how important it can be to talk to someone of a similar lived experience to you in therapy, and these are some great websites that can help you find Black and Asian therapists:

https://www.baatn.org.uk/

https://therapyforblackgirls.com/

https://www.blackmindsmatteruk.com/our-mission

https://sadgirlsclub.org/

https://www.inclusivetherapists.com/

SEXUAL ASSAULT

Rape Crisis offers different services to support you, including their National Telephone Helpline open from 12–12:30 p.m. and 7–9:30 p.m. every day of the year:

0808 802 9999.

https://rapecrisis.org.uk/

Resources

The Havens are specialist centres in London for people who have been raped or sexually assaulted. Their helpline is open twenty-four hours a day, seven days a week:

020 3299 6900

https://www.thehavens.org.uk/

DOMESTIC ABUSE

Refuge supports women and children experiencing domestic abuse and has a freephone, 24-hour National Domestic Abuse Helpline.

https://www.refuge.org.uk/

0808 2000 247

EATING DISORDERS

Beat Eating Disorders have plenty of information and resources to help you, and they also run a helpline open 365 days a year from 9 a.m. to 8 p.m. during the week and 4 p.m. to 8 p.m. on weekends and bank holidays.

https://www.beateatingdisorders.org.uk/support-services/helplines

0808 801 0677

Resources

BEREAVEMENT

Cruse bereavement care support those dealing with grief.

www.cruse.org.uk

0808 808 1677

DISCRIMINATION

Show Racism the Red Card is an anti-racism educational charity that uses workshops and training sessions, among other resources to combat racism.

https://www.theredcard.org/

Runnymede is the UK's leading independent race equality think tank, that generates resources to challenge race inequality in Britain.

https://www.runnymedetrust.org/

Stop Hate UK is a leading national organisation working to challenge all forms of Hate Crime and discrimination. They run a 24-hour help line for anyone who is a victim of a Hate Crime.

https://www.stophateuk.org/

0800 138 1625

Text: 07717 989 025